MORE WILDERNESS WALKS

MORE WILDERNESS WALKS

WALKS

CAMERON McNEISH & RICHARD ELSE

BBC

This book is published to accompany the television series entitled *Wilderness Walks*, which was first broadcast in 1998. The series was produced by Triple Echo Productions Limited for BBC Scotland.
Executive Producer: Neil Fraser
Producer-director: Richard Else

Published by BBC Worldwide Limited, Woodlands,
80 Wood Lane, London W12 0TT

First published 1998

ISBN 0 563 38450 6

Commissioning Editor: Nicky Copeland
Project Editor: Khadija Manjlai
Copy-editor: Hugh Morgan
Art Editor: Town Group Creative
Designer: Jane Coney
Cartographer: Chris Shaw

PICTURE CREDITS: Richard Else: 179, 202–203, 219; Ian Evans/Moutain Images: 2–3, 18–19, 22–23, 71; Alex Gillespie: 70; Alan Gordon: 74–75, 78–79, 79, 90–91, 91, 94–95, 98–99, 102–103, 110, 114–115, 122–123, 123, 126–127, 130–131, 134, 146, 147, 158–159, 159, 162–163, 166–167, 170, 174–175, 178–179, 182–183, 186–187, 198–199; Cameron McNeish: 51 (bottom), 211; David Paterson: 83, 142–143, 150, 194–195, 210–211, 214–215; Tom Prentice: 46; Scotland in Focus: 26–27, 27, 31, 38–39, 42–43, 43, 51 (top), 54–55, 58, 58–59, 62; Chris Townsend: 111.

Set in Goudy
Printed and bound in Great Britain by Butler & Tanner Limited, Frome and London
Colour separations by Radstock Reproductions Limited, Midsomer Norton
Jacket printed by Lawrence Allen Limited, Weston-super-Mare

PREVIOUS PAGES: BEN-DAMPH AND COULIN FOREST FROM LOCH DAMH

Contents

Preface

Once again our heartfelt thanks go to numerous friends and colleagues, without whose help this book, and the accompanying television series, could not have been accomplished. We would especially like to thank our commissioning editor at BBC Scotland, Neil Fraser (Head of Sport and Leisure), for his unflagging support and enthusiasm. It is a rare treat to have a commissioning editor who is also a dedicated hill man and someone who has brought to bear on the series a sharp eye and deep appreciation of the outdoors. Similarly, our thanks also go to another keen walker, Colin Cameron, BBC Scotland's Head of Production, for his continued commitment to this difficult area of broadcasting. Without their encouragement, and that of Brenda Macarthur, this project could not have been realized in the way we all hoped. Brenda's assistance is especially appreciated, and without her understanding of the hundred and one complexities of both book and television production this project would have been even more chaotic! This note would be incomplete without our acknowledging Nancy Braid, Val Henry and Ailsa Muirhead, who all played such an important role in bringing both television programmes and book to fruition. Without their insight into the complicated and murky world of finance, our packed lunches would have been all the poorer!

At BBC Worldwide we are indebted to our long-suffering editors Nicky Copeland and Khadija Manjlai; to copy-editor Hugh Morgan (now an expert in reading small-print Gaelic names from the Ordnance Survey maps); designer Jane Coney and picture researcher David Cottingham. By now they have all probably realized that working with authors who are inevitably 'out on the hill' when deadlines loom is a testing relationship, and both Cameron and I would like to thank them for their understanding and patience.

At Triple Echo Productions a special vote of appreciation goes to our Production Manager, Laura Hill, who has the unenviable task of organizing all the project logistics, and our Executive Producer, David Taylor, who has brought a fine editorial eye to bear on the films. Similarly, Margaret Wicks balanced the competing demands of research, book and television production in her characteristically imperturbable way; without her skilful insight into what is possible, slightly impossible and absolutely impossible, the whole enterprise would have grounded well before takeoff! We are most grateful to Chartech (producers of the Aqua 3 map protection system), Lowe Alpine, Salomon and Terra Nova for the use of their equipment during the writing of this book. All their products were subject to rigorous use in a wide variety of conditions and all performed extremely well.

Last, but by no stretch of the imagination least, we are conscious of the enormous contribution made by our guests who have shared their insights into the importance of our wild places. Similarly, we have been delighted to meet so many viewers and readers, whether at slide shows or on the hill itself. It is your kind comments and continued support that has proved such a valuable encouragement when struggling through bogs (a particular dislike of Cameron's) or experiencing one of Scotland's unusual bad weather days! For both of us, writing this book has been a labour of love and has resulted in some of our finest days in the hills. We hope that enjoyment is not purely limited to its making but that in the reading of it a similar pleasure is re-created.

Cameron McNeish and Richard Else

INTRODUCTION

•

Cameron McNeish

One of the undoubted privileges of presenting the BBC2 television series *Wilderness Walks* has been the opportunity to probe into the psyche of my guests. This hasn't wholly been a pandering to my own inquisitive nature or an attempt to put folk in an embarrassing situation, but an opportunity to discover how wild places – forests and mountains, deserts and Arctic ice – have affected them as people, and in some cases have influenced their entire way of life. All of them would agree that the wilderness experience has, in some way, changed them for the better.

Let me give an example. One of my guests suggested that a positive wilderness experience can be seen as a microcosm of what an ecologically aware lifestyle can be. If you take, for instance, environmentally sound methods for handling waste products in wild places, those methods serve as a model that results in a more responsible attitude to handling waste materials at home. Similarly, moving through the landscape in what American outdoorsman Ray Jardine calls the Fox Walk teaches you to be much more observant, using your peripheral vision to see things that you would normally pass without any notice. Such skills of observation have obvious benefit when taken from the wilderness and used in our everyday urban environment.

Wild areas have long been recognized as places where we can replenish ourselves, where we can be refreshed by the beauty and wonder of them all, but Scottish mountaineer Hamish Brown takes that a stage further. In his book *The Last Hundred*, he writes: 'Slowly the hills turned pink and the shadows rose with dusk over their slopes. The first star shone out over a lemon-lined crest. At such moments we worship – and few but the mountaineer know the benediction of that long content.'

Hamish is probably right, but increasing numbers of people are recognizing wilderness as their land of *lost* content.

Current thinking suggests that something of a sea change is taking place in our attitude to the outdoors. For decades we have taken our technical creativity from the cities to the wild places. With our 50-pound (23-kg) backpacks ironically full of 'lightweight' gear, we have tried to 'conquer' nature; we've seen the mountains as a challenge, our long-distance trails as a racetrack and our equipment as a means of moving faster, higher and safer. In effect we've taken the ideas and ideals from the city in an attempt to live in the natural world the way we would at home. But now more and more people are recognizing that nature can teach us valuable lessons about how to live in our urban environments. That land of lost content can be our guide to greater harmony, even within the boundaries of our towns and cities.

Educationalists often speak of 'the teachable moment'; some may call it 'opportunity teaching'. It refers to a person's increased interest in a certain subject because the information being taught affects them directly at that particular moment in time. For example, a lecture on the High Atlas Mountains of Morocco is particularly well received by someone who is heading there the following week. Likewise, a wilderness walk can embrace dozens of teachable moments in which the message of living responsibly on the earth can be put across with great effectiveness. 'Learn of the green world what can be thy place,' wrote Ezra Pound.

In this postmodernist era we are realizing something of vital importance: while we probably know infinately more about the universe than our ancestors did, they knew something more essential about it than we do, something that curiously escapes us. I believe it's a spirituality that existed when we lived in harmony with nature, a deep understanding that our ancestors cherished, but one that we, standing on the threshold of a new millennium, have allowed to wither and atrophy.

For most of us, urban living has broken the tie we once had with the land. When was the last time you crumbled raw earth in your fingertips? When was the last time you washed your face in the dew? Even many of our farmers, those you would think are still deeply embedded in the ways of the earth, are invariably at odds with the land because of their modern agrochemical practices.

It looks a gloomy picture, but not all is lost.

It's heartening that people like Ray Jardine are rediscovering incredible truths about our links with the natural world from native American Indian sources, or that Hamish Brown has discovered in the Berber mountain people of Morocco a fundamental root in the natural world that makes them completely at home in what is essentially a harsh and unforgiving environment. As he has learnt from them, so can we. But perhaps the most important discovery of all is the understanding that anyone who spends any reasonable amount of time in the wild places will recognize that he or she is not irrevocably removed from the ways of the green world. In his fascinating book *The Great Blue Dream*, mountaineer Robert Leonard Reid writes:

> *I cannot leave the mountain behind when I return to the lowlands. It is this inability to separate mountain climber from urban dweller which convinces me that the Euroamerican's much-heralded break with nature is more a myth than reality. Our roots still reach deeply into the earth beneath us, but in an illusory world that appears increasingly human-made and human-controlled this elemental connection is easily forgotten.*

I suspect that many people who go to wilderness places still experience the resonances of man's bond with nature, still hear the echoes of the land's call on our lives.

Through the making of our television programmes, and through the writing of this book, Richard and I would dearly love to think that we might furnish a reminder of that elemental connection; that we are part of the web of life that we tritely call nature, connected to the rock and the air and the water of pre-life.

As in the first volume of *Wilderness Walks* we have described twelve walks, all in Scotland, that we believe portray something of the tremendous variety this small country has to offer. From the relatively benign landscape of the Scottish Borders we visit the surreal environment of the Trotternish ridge on Skye, and take in the high tops of Glen Nevis, Glen Affric, Torridon and the incredible hills of the far north-west. We wander the glens of the Cairngorms, indulge in the romantic history of the Trossachs and make our way through some of the hardest terrain in the country over the small, but incredibly tough, Galloway hills. All the routes desribed are in their own peculiar way pathways, down which we can return to some semblance of aware-ness of who we are, and where we have come from. We also hope that these routes into the timelessness of the natural world will enrich you, just as they have enriched us.

Access in Scotland

All the land we've walked over and written about is owned by someone, and the current law of the land expects us to respect that fact. It has always been under-stood that in Scotland the hillgoer, mountaineer or backpacker has enjoyed a moral right of freedom to roam in wild places, provided that he or she exercises good country-side manners and respect for those other activities also carried out in these wild areas, such as deerstalking and grouse-shooting.

The law in Scotland at present specifies that a trespass has been committed by a person who goes onto land owned or occupied by another without that person's consent and without having a right to do so. But a simple trespass such as this is not enshrined in statute as a criminal offence, so there cannot be a prosecution. The owner or occupier of the property must either obtain an interdict or, if damage to property has occurred, raise an action for damages. Additionally, a 'trespasser' may be asked by the owner or occupier to leave the property and, in the event of that person refusing to leave, the owner or occu-pier has the right to use 'reasonable force' to make him or her leave. There is no further definition of reasonable force, and one would imagine that any form of force, in this day and age, would invite allegations of assault. Scottish trespass is very much a grey area.

The Criminal Justice Act 1995 makes 'aggravated access' a criminal act, but the landowner or his agent must be able to prove that the person has come onto the land with the deliberate intention of disrupting the lawful activity of the estate.

Having said all that, the public and landowners widely accept that walkers, climbers and backpackers are more or less free to roam the upland areas of the Scottish

Highlands without undue restriction, and any impingement of that *de facto* right would undoubtedly create considerable public outcry.

Most estates in the Highlands and Islands are involved in deerstalking and ask hill-goers to respect the stag-shooting season, which generally runs from 20 August to 20 October. Often a chat with the keeper or factor can tell you where shooting will be taking place, leaving you free to go and walk a different route across the estate. Sometimes a keeper can tell you of a better route than the one you've planned. Bear in mind that while many disagree with the whole concept of hunting and shooting, such sport does exist and many estates claim to earn a large part of their annual income from stalking. The alternative, however much we may feel disinclined towards such blood sports, could well be something considerably more unpleasant, like mass coniferization.

The low-impact backpacker, walking solo or in a small group of two or maybe three, taking photographs and leaving only the odd footprint as a sign of his passing, is little threat to any landowner or blood sports enthusiast, and is a fine example to others.

The Munro Game

In 1890 a soldier and diplomat by the name of Sir Hugh Munro, of Lindertis in Angus, compiled a list of the 3000-foot (914-m) mountains in Scotland. In the list, published in the *Scottish Mountaineering Club Journal*, he claimed that 538 tops were over 3000 feet, 283 of which he believed merited status as 'separate mountains'. (There has always been much speculation about the criteria for deciding what separates a 'top' from a 'mountain'. In 1933 J. Gall Inglis, then editor of *Munro's Tables*, suggested that there should be a drop of 75–100 feet (23–31 m) between mountains, but to date there has been no firm guideline on what constitutes a 'mountain'. Munro himself was in favour of updating only when maps were re-surveyed and revised.)

Almost as soon as Munro had published his first list, the Ordnance Survey published its revised six-inch maps of Scotland and obvious discrepancies were found in Munro's tabulations. Immediately, he began revising his tables but sadly died in 1919, aged 63, before they were published. J.R. Young and A.W. Peacock, fellow members of the SMC, took on the task and, working from Munro's notes, produced revised tables in 1921. Since then, following various OS surveys and revisions of the tables, the number of 'official' Munros has settled at 284.

In recent years it has become almost fashionable to take up Munro-bagging, attempting to climb all 284 mountains. Some folk take a lifetime to achieve the round; others take on the challenge as a major expedition of a lifetime and climb them all in three or four months. To date the Munros have been climbed in 51 days (the fastest), during the months of the winter equinox (Martin Moran in 1984–5) and with a mountain bike!

The Scottish Mountaineering Club keeps a list of all those who have 'compleated' (sic) the round of Munros. The present 'keeper' of those records is Dr C.M. Huntley, Old Medwyn, Spittal, Carnwath, Lanarkshire ML11 8LY. At the time of writing there are about 1800 Munroists on the list.

While the Munros, as they are now known, comprise 284 Scottish mountains which lift their heads over the 3000-foot (914-m) contour, the Corbetts, named after John Rooke Corbett, make up another 220 separate hills over 2500 feet (764 m) scattered at random throughout southern Scotland and the Highlands and Islands.

Mountain Safety

Appropriate safety precautions must always be taken when venturing onto the Scottish hills. Don't set off without waterproofs and spare clothing, even in summer, and food, a map, compass, whistle and torch are vital items of equipment. Scottish winter conditions are often Arctic in nature and just as severe as those found on higher European mountains. Such conditions must be treated with respect; an ice-axe, crampons and specialist winter gear are essential, as is an understanding of snow conditions, including avalanches and cornices. Everyone venturing onto the Scottish hills in winter should be able to navigate accurately, especially as the weather changes extremely abruptly. Remember there is no such thing as Scottish winter hill-walking – in the normal conditions of a Scottish winter the activity is no less than mountaineering – so if you don't feel competent in your ability as a mountaineer, stay low down. Even better, enrol with one of the Scottish climbing courses which are offered by numerous qualified instructors and organizations in the Highlands.

And when you do finally set off on your wilderness discovery trip, let someone know where you are going and when you will return. Every year search-parties waste countless hours looking for people in the wrong places – so write out a brief description of your route and when you will return and leave it with a responsible person, a policeman, a landlady or your loved ones at home. The appreciation of our wild lands is heightened by the peace of mind that comes with knowing that if something should go drastically wrong, at least the rescue teams will know where to look for you.

CHAPTER ONE

THE BORDERS

FOLLOWING THE SONGLINES

•

Cameron McNeish

A three-day walk from Moffat to Galashiels

MAP: *OS 1:50 000 Sheets 73, 78 and 79*
START: *Moffat. Grid Ref: 092051*
FINISH: *Galashiels. Grid Ref: 492358*
LENGTH: *45 miles (72 km)*
APPROXIMATE TIME: *3 days*
TERRAIN: *Good footpaths and tracks all the way. Follows the route of the Southern Upland Way and is waymarked by an acorn symbol*
ACCOMMODATION: *Hotels, guest-houses and b&bs in Moffat, Traquair and Galashiels. Youth hostels at Broadmeadows, near Yarrowford*

Just as much of my knowledge of Ireland stems from the folk-music of that country, so my knowledge of the Scottish Borders stems from the ballads and songs of the region. And if there's one area of the Borders whose very name is capable of stirring the heart-strings of emotion it is Ettrick – the Ettrick Forest of the lawless and the hunted, the Ettrick Forest of the royal hunts, the Ettrick Forest of song and story.

My wife Gina and I wanted to visit Ettrick and had considered a high-level round of the Ettrick Valley itself, a good 22-mile (35-km) jaunt. Either that or visit the northern Ettrick tops as part of a 35-mile (56-km) walk from Peebles to Moffat. Instead, we opted for a 45-mile (72-km) route between Moffat and Galashiels, taking a taxi to Moffat, then walking back to the car in Galashiels via the Southern Upland Way. This route would take us below the excellent Bodesbeck Ridge, from Bodesbeck Law to Herman Law, with an option actually to traverse the ridge if time permitted, and the historical Minch Moor, from Traquair to Galashiels, a high-level route that follows the steps of cattle-drovers, battling dukes and kings.

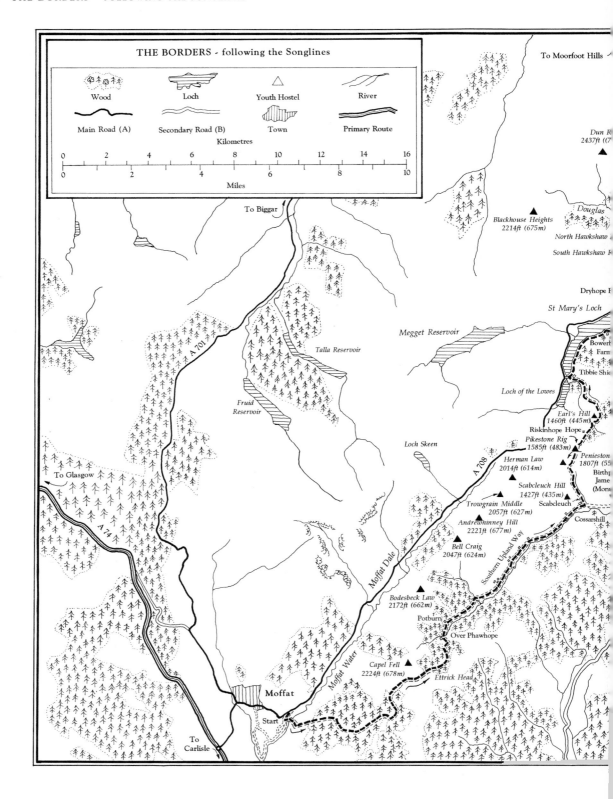

THE BORDERS - following the Songlines

Wood   Loch   Youth Hostel   River

Main Road (A)   Secondary Road (B)   Town   Primary Route

Kilometres

0   2   4   6   8   10   12   14   16

0   2   4   6   8   10

Miles

To Moorfoot Hills

To Biggar

Dun R
2437ft (7

Blackhouse Heights
2214ft (675m)

Douglas

North Hawkshaw

South Hawkshaw F

Dryhope F

St Mary's Loch

Megget Reservoir

Bower
Farm

Tibbie Shie

Loch of the Lowes

Talla Reservoir

Fruid
Reservoir

Earl's Hill
1460ft (445m)

Riskinhope Hope

Loch Skeen

Pikestone Rig
1585ft (483m)

Penieston
1807ft (55

Birth
Jame
(Mon

Herman Law
2014ft (614m)

A 701

To Glasgow

Scabcleuch Hill
1427ft (435m)

Scabcleuch

Trowgrain Middle
2057ft (627m)

Cossarshill

Andrewhinney Hill
2221ft (677m)

A 74

Bell Craig
2047ft (624m)

Moffat Dale

Bodesbeck Law
2172ft (662m)

Potburn

Over Phawhope

Moffat Water

Capel Fell
2224ft (678m)

Moffat

Start

Ettrick Head

To
Carlisle

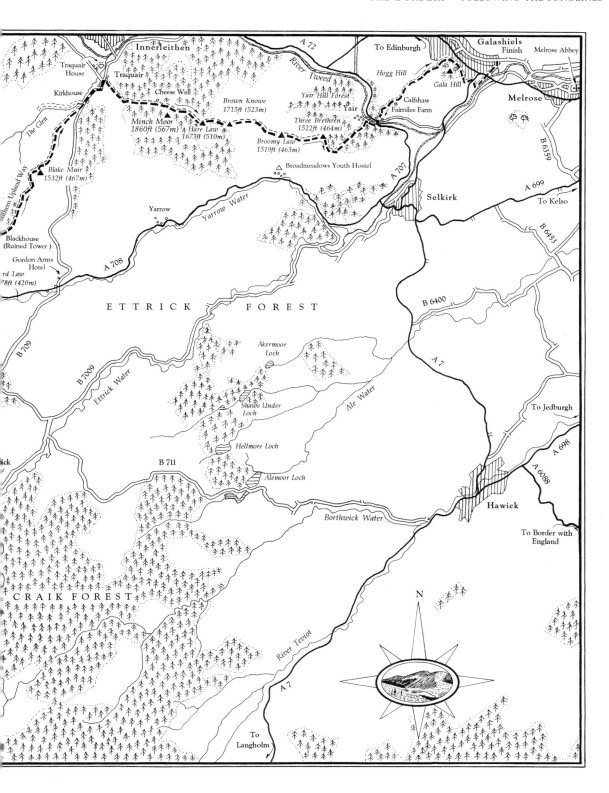

Traquair House
Innerleithen
A 72
River Tweed
To Edinburgh
Galashiels
Finish
Melrose Abbey
Traquair
Hogg Hill
Gala Hill
Kirkhouse
Cheese Well
Brown Knowe
1715ft (523m)
Yair Hill Forest
Yair
Calfshaw
Fairnilee Farm
Melrose
The Glen
Minch Moor
1860ft (567m)
Hare Law
1673ft (510m)
Three Brethren
1522ft (464m)
B 6359
Broomy Law
1519ft (463m)
Southern Upland Way
Blake Muir
1532ft (467m)
Broadmeadows Youth Hostel
A 707
Selkirk
A 699
To Kelso
Yarrow
Yarrow Water
Blackhouse
(Ruined Tower)
B 6453
Gordon Arms
Hotel
rd Law
78ft (420m)
A 708
E T T R I C K   F O R E S T
B 6400
B 709
Akermoor
Loch
A 7
B 7009
Ettrick Water
Shaws Under
Loch
Ale Water
To Jedburgh
A 698
Hellmore Loch
A 6088
B 711
Alemoor Loch
Hawick
Borthwick Water
To Border with
England
C R A I K   F O R E S T
N
River Teviot
A 7
To
Langholm

One might argue that a route like this, rarely more than a couple of hours from a road, could never be described as wilderness, but the word itself is difficult to define. I would dare suggest that the word is more of an adjective than a noun, and essentially defines a quality that produces a particular mood or feeling in a given individual.

In this respect, especially when walking a route where the historical aspects are almost tangible, areas like Ettrick and Minch Moor are so heavily weighted with meaning of a symbolic and, for me, a personal kind that you can feel you have been transported back several centuries to when this part of Scotland was truly wild, rugged and remote. It was this spirit of place that I wanted to examine on this three-day journey. I was also keen to explore another curious phenomenon.

The late Bruce Chatwin, one of the finest travel writers I have read, once wrote about the link between the physical world that Australian Aborigines live in and a parallel world from which they believe their physical world is derived. This other world is their 'Dreamtime', and for them it is as real as the physical world in which they live. What I found intriguing is that the Aborigines believe their ancestors created the natural world by *singing* it into being.

The songs the ancestors sang created the land itself – and the animals, the birds, the plants and the creeks – and modern Aborigines habitually go walkabout to experience these 'songlines', what they call the Footsteps of the Ancestors. By singing the old songs they believe they can play a vital part in the continuing creation. I think it's a lovely concept, and it's not as far removed from traditional Christian thinking as you'd perhaps think. Michael Mayne, Dean of Westminster, in his superb book *This Sunrise of Wonder*, writes:

> *I think of Caedmon, who died in 680 and who is memorialized in Poet's Corner in the Abbey as the first known poet of Anglo-Saxon England. He was a cowherd in the employ of the Abbess Hilda of Whitby, and one night he had a dream in which he was commanded to sing. He replied that he was poor and useless and that singing was not in his line. 'Sing', he was told, and when he asked what he should sing he was told to sing of those things he knew instinctively: he was told to sing of the glories of creation.*

How many of us have had our spirits so lifted by some glorious manifestation of creation that we have burst into song? And how many songs and ballads from areas like Ireland or the Scottish Borders have been influenced by the sheer magnificence of those areas, or by some historical event – a battle, a jilted lover, or some other event? I wanted to experience the songlines of the Borders.

We had booked a taxi in advance, but the driver was 20 minutes late in picking us up. I tried to engage him in conversation but once we had run the gamut of the weather (which, incidentally, was absolutely superb), the local job situation (dire, he reckoned: most of the woollen mills were run down years ago and electronics is now the big industry – silicone dale? The last stronghold of the woollen/knitting/weaving industry is Hawick, and apparently things are pretty desperate there too) and the pros and cons of the taxi-hire business we fell into a mutually agreeable silence. Gina dozed happily in the back seat while mentally I went through our itinerary for the hundredth time. I knew roughly where I wanted to begin walking – about a mile south of Moffat. Although I can't say I knew the Borders with any sense of conviction, I felt I had studied the map enough times to make a good stab at a reasonable route. As it happened, the taxi overran the place where I thought we wanted to be dropped off by about a mile! Ho-hum!

Moffat to Scabcleuch

Taxi duly paid (it cost about £30, late 1997 prices), we walked back a mile, amazed how hot it was under the November sun. Our humour was good now that we were walking, and we were delighted with the weather – back along the road, down a side road and up the muddy side of a plantation to reach a forestry track. Moffat looked good in the distance, church spires and roofs caught amid a jumble of low, rounded hills.

Forest-walking can be boring; there's not all that much to look at once you've had your fill of lodgepole pines and conifers. Surprisingly, we passed a house, like a keeper's house, surrounded on all sides by dense green plantations, with no view at all. What keeps someone living in such a place? Love of solitude? But surely part of solitude is being able to enjoy the landscape around you and being able to appreciate it without the blemishes of mankind. Can you appreciate trees, trees and nothing but trees? Not for me.

Thankfully, we soon escaped the trees. A footpath bore off to the left running up a rather wide forest ride. A stream roared its way down the length of it, swollen by the recent rainy weather. We were still rising and it wasn't long before we left the trees behind for a very different landscape. We reached a large round sheep enclosure, known in this part of Scotland as a 'fank', beyond which the ground seemed to fall away into a prominent cleuch. (In this part of the world a cleuch is a steep-sided glen.) The slopes were eroded and bare and we took a rising traverse along our side of the valley. As the ascent began to ease off, a footbridge took us to another short climb, this time onto a peaty col – Ettrick Head, on the very watershed of Scotland, where the peat-coloured waters oozed from beneath the feet to form the nascent headwaters of the River Tweed, one of the mighty rivers of Scotland.

This is how I expected Ettrick to be. Secretive saucers in the hills, winding high-level valleys where a man could hide out and never be found, high rolling hills with long views where enemy forces could be seen at great distances. This was the heart of Ettrick.

WALKERS LEAVING ETTRICK HEAD, THE HEART OF ETTRICK DEER FOREST

•

Ettrick – a name that excites the wanderer in me, a bit like Torridon or Applecross. Curiously, the place has virtually nothing physically in common with these highland areas, but it does have a parallel in its resonances of wildness and remoteness. Wasn't this the Ettrick Forest that sheltered patriot William Wallace when he survived as an outlaw in the late thirteenth century? And the Bruce? Didn't the Black Douglas and, later, the Marquis of Montrose haunt this same lofty fastness when they too were being hunted like wild animals? An ancient verse proclaims:

> *The Ettrick Foreste is a feir firests.*
> *In it grows mony a semelie tree.*
> *There's hart and hinde, and dae and rae*
> *And a' wild beasts in grete plentie.*

As the verse suggests, the Ettrick Forest later became a deer forest, a place where the royals could hunt game rather than outlaws, but like much of Scotland it also became a grazing ground for the ubiquitous sheep and it was here that the poet James Hogg was born, possibly the best-known shepherd of all.

James Hogg, the Ettrick Shepherd, lived from 1770 to 1835 and is widely remembered in Scotland as a contemporary of Robert Burns. Like Burns, Hogg came from a working background and it's thought that his rise to prominence as a poet was due to the patronage of Sir Walter Scott. Scott travelled widely as Sheriff of Selkirkshire, and he often met Hogg and enjoyed his company in drinking dens like Tibbie Shiels Inn near St Mary's Loch and the Gordon Arms on Yarrow Water. Under Scott's patronage, Hogg found his way into print. Today, although many people have heard of Hogg, very few are familiar with his work. His best-known prose work is probably *The Private Memoirs and Confessions of a Justified Sinner* – a tremendous title for what Roger Smith, author of the official guide to the Southern Upland Way and Walking Development Officer of Borders Council, describes as 'an astonishing psychological thriller way ahead of its time'.

Today, the Ettrick Forest has been tamed by a road that runs to its head. Conifer plantations cloak the hillsides in great rectangular shrouds, but high on the tops lingers a hint, a whisper, of its former glory. Blue hills rolling out in every direction, we sat by the stile on Ettrick Head, the boundary fence between Dumfries & Galloway and Borders regions, and watched a short-eared owl quarter the ground searching for prey. We listened to the voice of the wind and the occasional guttural 'goback, goback, goback' call of grouse. Time stands still in places like this, as James Hogg himself experienced when he witnessed the apparition of a drove of Highland cattle accompanied by three drovers.

'It is quite evident,' he later wrote, 'that we must attribute these appearances to particular states of the atmosphere, and suppose them to be shadows of realities; the airy resemblance of scenes passing in distant parts of the country, and by some singular operation of natural causes thus expressively imaged in the acclivities of the mountains.'

Could there be a resonance here of the Aboriginal Dreamtime, the parallel world of the Aborigines' ancestors? Such apparitions are not uncommon in the mountains. Didn't the mountaineer and writer Frank Smythe experience a very similar thing in the mountains of Kintail when he witnessed a massacre that must have taken place over 200 years before? Modern walkers, too, have told of such curious experiences. A close friend of mine swears that he heard the tread of marching feet and the rumble of chariots near Hadrian's Wall in Northumberland. He was too terrified to look out of his tent. Did these people see ghosts, or is there some quantum physics concept of the simultaneous nature of time – past, present and future – that we don't yet understand?

I had originally wanted to walk over the high tops to Scabcleuch, a long ridge of rounded tops which runs along the southern side of Moffat Dale, but the hour was against us. By the time we walked up to the first of the tops it would have been getting dark, and it was still a good seven or eight miles (eleven to thirteen km) to Scabcleuch. We decided to walk down the length of the Ettrick Valley. From Moffat to Scabcleuch via Ettrick Head, Capel Fell, White Shank, Bodesbeck Law, Bell Craig, Andrewhinney Hill, Trowgrain Middle, Herman Law and Peniestone Knowe is a big day, about 17 miles (27 km) of rough, trackless walking.

From Ettrick Head we dropped back into the forest and a forest track, but not the dense, suffocating forestry of earlier. There was an openness now and we could see the farm buildings at Potburn down the valley. It wasn't long before we could see a building even closer to us: the bothy at Over Phawhope.

Seduced by the peace of the place, we stopped for a brew. I took a wander around the building while Gina enjoyed her own space inside. I tried to imagine what it must have been like here in the twelfth and thirteenth centuries when Wallace, the Bruce and the Douglas came here as hunted men, finding sanctuary amid these high places. I suppose the whole valley would have been forested, but cloaked in a very different kind of forest – oak, birch, rowan, juniper and Scots pine – and, of course, the wildlife that went with such a forest: wild boar, wolves, deer and possibly bears.

These thoughts and stirrings were still with me as we began the five-mile (eight-km) walk down the valley, imaginings that were soon fired by the dimming sky and the first stars. As the great blocks of forestry were lost in the gloaming and as the occasional houses we passed were shrunk by the darkness into vague shapes, I felt something of the spirit of Ettrick, that persona that never dies no matter how we physically change it, like Sandwood Bay, or Doune in Knoydart or Glen Coe. Does landscape have a spirit? I suspect that in certain places it does, a spirit spawned by past events and occurrences, even if those events and occurrences happen only in your own mind.

Road-walking is hard on the body. I don't believe we were ever made to take the

St Mary's Loch, half-way point of the route and one of the best-loved
stretches of water in the Borders

•

sort of pounding that tarmac gives, and it was with some relief that we checked the map at a place called Cossarshill – Scabcleuch was less than a mile away, and indeed we could see the lights of the house through the trees. I'd been here before, on a spring day with my son Gordon when we visited Ettrick Kirk and the graveyard of James Hogg. We had walked from the kirk up to the foot of Peniestone Knowe and back down Scabcleuch. That knowledge was now to prove helpful as we walked up the path in the dark, our headtorch batteries fading. A shepherd came out of the house at the bottom to check on us. 'We're heading over to St Mary's Loch,' I volunteered to his unasked question of where we were going. 'Yer mad going over there in the dark,' he answered. 'We're well experienced,' I replied quickly and then, to change the subject, 'Will the weather hold, do you think?' He brightened considerably at this. 'Aye it's looking grand.' There didn't seem much more to be said now that we seemed to have his tacit approval, so I waved a goodbye. He hadn't quite given up, but his humour was better now. 'If ye've no showed up at Tibbie Shiels by Monday we'll get someone to come and look for ye,' he shouted after us, but with a laugh this time. I didn't want to tell him we were going to camp less than a mile from his house.

We pitched the tent on a flat sward high up on the pass. It was a good night, starlit, still and mild. Gina was sound asleep by eight. It wasn't much later when I followed suit.

Scabcleuch to Traquair

There was an eerie stillness in the morning. I woke at about seven and could barely see the reeds in front of the tent. An hour later it was lighter, but a thin mist obscured everything. The morning had the feel of summer before the sun burns its way through the mists. We knew instinctively that this wouldn't happen in November, but something in the atmosphere encouraged us and put a spring in our step as we moved off up towards the pass.

We were on the old Kirk Road, the ancient path from St Mary's Loch formerly taken by worshippers treading the five miles (eight km) to church on a Sunday morning. A ten-mile (sixteen-km) round trip over a pass 1500 feet (457 m) high puts a perspective on the spiritual commitment of folk a hundred years ago. Was it passion that drove them to this sort of dedication to worship, was it superstition, or could it have been fear? – fear of being outcast by their contemporaries? Fear of the minister and his inevitable tongue-lashing? Fear of eternal hell and brimstone they would face if they became backslidden? I like to think of them wandering over here light of foot, spiritually uplifted and expectant of meeting with their Lord in that tiny little kirk, but I suspect I'm being overly romantic. To be honest, I have difficulty in believing that people walked this distance to church – could this not be an old coffin route, the path used by funeral processions to the nearest consecrated ground?

Once over the pass we followed the Southern Upland Way diversion off the eastern side of Pikestone Rig towards Riskinhope Hope, an old sheep farm of which only a few crumbling walls remain, a deserted spot complete with an indefinable air of melancholy. Dry-stone wall boundaries still marked out the fields tilting up steep slopes on both sides of the old steading. Nettles clustered around the crooked portals of the old door. 'Hope' in this part of Scotland means a valley with a meandering burn and has nothing to do with expectation or optimism.

Curiously, despite the dereliction I could sense its spirit of the past: a little spot among the folds in the hills where people were born and died, laughed and cried, rejoiced and were saddened, worked and made play. Could there be something of these human emotions which are for ever bound up in the ether of a place? I've experienced this same sense of a tangible past in deserted Himalayan villages close to the Tibetan border, in ancient settlements in Tunisia and Morocco, and in countless locations throughout the Highlands of Scotland. Can the strength and power of such strong human emotions, like the sadness of leaving a lovely spot like this, of allowing the house to fall into dereliction, be channelled into something that is bound up for ever in those ruins, in the land – a soul, a spirit that pervades the ambience of the place for years, for centuries, to come? A spirit of place?

My good friend Jim Perrin describes it well:

Times come when it is proper to still yourself and go down into the profound interplay of consciousness where common humanity, human history and something beyond both of those inform each other. On the coast of Llyn I know a set of steps cut once into the rock and smoothed by centuries of feet. They lead down to the wave margin and to a well. If you listen, the clamour of voices here, of wave-sound, tide race, the stilled pre-Cambrian magma – a drowned girl's scream, a pilgrim's prayer, slap of a launched coracle, the crack and hiss of cooling rock – are coexistent along the flicker of time. It happened here, and so much else besides. The distillation of these events is the spirit of the place.

Could it be that in certain situations past, present and future can simply fuse together, or is it simply that in our fast-paced and furious world we subliminally long for the simpler, quieter way of life which such old places suggest to us? A nostalgic longing for former, simpler times?

Gina sat quietly by the ruined gable end and I was grateful for her silence. I felt moved by this simple place and saddened too. Some lovely old Scots pine trees, which once protected this very house from the elements, were in their final death throes. Like the ruined house, many of them were also in the past tense, blown down by those very winds they had stood against for years. Several still stood but they were geriatric,

Above: The Three Brethren, at the end of the Minch Moor ridge

Right: Evening falls on the summit of Minch Moor

•

and like so many stands of pine all over the country they suffered from the croak factor: as the old ones die, no youngsters take their place. So many of our forests form a geriatric community, with no saplings, no young trees, only the old and the dying. The ruination of those trees that once protected the place cast a shadow. I looked closely at the ground – no seedlings, no new shoots. Only the rocks remained, and the spirit. Why should this be so? It's ironic, but the very sheep that were fostered in a place like this have been the ruination of those trees. The saplings have been eaten, browsed, by the ubiquitous black-faced yowes, the woolly locusts of the countryside.

> *Ca' the yowes, tae the knowes,*
> *Ca' them whaur the burnie flows,*
> *Ca' them whaur the heather grows,*
> *My bonnie dearie.*

A short climb took us around the back of a wee hillock called Earl's Hill and down by the Captain's Road, an old drovers' road that runs down to Tibbie Shiels Inn by St Mary's Loch. James Hogg and his socialite friend Sir Walter Scott met here often. The local hoi polloi didn't like it when Hogg referred to the great writer as Wattie, although Scott didn't seem to mind. We didn't linger at the inn, although Gina was keen to stop for a coffee. I suspect my mind was still at Riskinhope Hope, still wrestling with the changes in our countryside and the different landscape values we have. I didn't particularly want to be with people.

Instead, I promised Gina an early lunch, and we made our way along the southern shore of St Mary's Loch, past the modern sailing clubhouse and down a narrow muddy path. A stand of deciduous trees broke the monotony of the path, a stand of trees which again lacked any regeneration, and then we were back beside the choking monoculture of modern forestry, past Bowerhope Farm and along to the far end of the loch. It was cold and damp beside the water's edge, and after stopping for the promised picnic lunch we were eager to be on our way again, an eagerness driven by the damp chill in the air.

It took me a good 30 minutes to warm up, and that was subconsciously helped by the fact that the sun was desperately trying to break through the low-lying cloud. We crossed the A708 Selkirk to Moffat road and climbed steadily uphill through a field past Dryhope Farm and its ruined towerhouse. The Borders area is rich in such antiquity and has a real aura of the past, much more than I've experienced in the Highlands. It's here in the ruins and the placenames that you feel the region's history.

From Dryhope the route lay uphill over a relatively low pass between Ward Law and South Hawkshaw Rig. A dumpy hill on our right, like a moraine, was marked on the map as an earthwork. We were in fact now contouring the eastern slopes of South Hawkshaw and North Hawkshaw Rigs, a wide and open area that steadily closed in to where the Douglas Burn, named after the infamous Border fighting family, runs down from its headwaters betweeen Blackhouse Heights and Dun Rig, a lonely and desolate spot. Dun would suggest an ancient fort and Blackhouse Heights is obviously associated with the house and ruined castle we were about to pass.

The Border family of Douglas was traditionally known as the Black Douglas, not only because of their swarthy appearance but because of their reputation among their enemies.

> It fell upon the Lammastime, when Muir men win their hay,
> The doughty Douglas bore them to ride to England to make a fray,
> They took the Gordons and the Grahams, the Lindsays so fine and free,
> But the Jardines would not wi' them ride and they rue it to this day.

The ruined castle is called Blackhouse appropriately and an older tower on the site is thought to have been the home of Sir James Douglas, who fought alongside Robert the Bruce during the wars of independence in the early fourteenth century and who carried the Bruce's heart to the Crusades before burying it in the graveyard of Melrose Abbey, where it lies today. Very little is left of the ruins, choked with trees, and a modern farmhouse is immediately adjacent to it. Some distance behind stands another house, a dour building also appropriately called Blackhouse.

A long uphill pull soon lifted us high beyond the houses and into the forest again, but not for long. Soon, distant views opened up beyond the trees and we were enjoying the sudden spaciousness and open skies. Leaving the forest behind at a fence, we could see our track winding gently up and down over the rounded breasts of Blake Muir, the grassy slopes falling away on either side to deep valleys, with the distant Moorfoots and Minch Moor, our route for the following day, coming into view. We took this high road in silence, lost in our own thoughts and enjoying the skies and the distant vistas. There is a real delight in being up high, losing little height as the track gently winds its way into little grooves and cols. All too soon we began the long descent with the valley called The Glen to our left. To the right, the bald pate of Minch Moor peaked beyond its forested slopes, and other hills led the eye down to the rounded top of Mountbenger Law. At a farm at its foot James Hogg had a pretty unsuccessful time as a farmer.

The last of the light was going when we reached Kirkhouse and passed the church on the road leading to Traquair. No time to visit Traquair House as we wanted to get fairly high into the forest before camping. Every mile we walked this evening would save us time tomorrow.

A farm road led us out of Traquair in the dark, and we climbed steadily, putting off the moment when we had to switch on our headtorches. Gina was tired now, and when we reached a forest road junction we took the opportunity of available water, and a flat, stony bit of ground. It was good to stop, with the lights of Traquair and Innerleithen lighting up the skies to the north.

Traquair to Galashiels

•

Daylight broke on a grey, misty morning with a cool breeze blowing from the south-west. We had slept well and were keen to be away early for the final dozen or so miles to Galashiels. It was a steady pull up onto Minch Moor, but the antiquity of the track we were following was plain to see. Old cobbles showed clearly through the mud and the lichens, and it was sad, higher up, to see where forestry vehicles had ripped up the cobbles with little reverence for their history. Edward I had marched along this road on his way to conquer Scotland – the Wallace and the Bruce had used it, as had the Marquis of Montrose fleeing from the Battle of Philiphaugh. It's said he rattled on the doors of Traquair House seeking shelter but wasn't allowed entry! Drovers also used this route, and near the summit of the moor two curious stones mark the spot known as the Cheese Well where drovers once sprinkled a few crumbs of food to appease the little people who were guardians of the high and exposed Minch Moor road.

A series of ups and downs took us over Hare Law and Brown Knowe, with its cairn made from stones from a broken wall, around the north of Broomy Law (I wonder if this is where Glasgow's Broomielaw comes from). All this time we saw barely more than a few feet in front of us – it was cold and damp too. Dropping down to the east of Broomy Law we came out of the cloud and along a sheltered path beside a forest plantation before climbing again to the Three Brethren, three tall cairns that stand in Selkirk Burgh, Yair and Bowhill. The summit of the Three Brethren is on the route of Selkirk's Common Riding, an annual event that sees a cavalcade of horseriders go around the bounds, or the marches, of Selkirk Burgh.

In 1931 a party of Scottish Youth Hostel Association officials crossed Minch Moor to Broadmeadows to open Scotland's first youth hostel. They were followed 50 years later by another party, this time celebrating the association's golden jubilee. Many walkers and ramblers stay at hostels like those at Broadmeadows, Loch Ossian, Carn Dearg and Glen Affric, which still exist to fly the flag for people who like the idea of 'cheap, simple accommodation in wild areas', to use a phrase of the movement's founder, Richard Schirmann.

Again, we didn't linger and dropped down the stony Southern Upland Way track into the Yair Hill Forest. At one point three motorcyclists roared up from the Yarrow Valley below us, shattering the silence and leaving behind a heavy smell of petrol – high-octane disturbance and signs that we were approaching civilization again. For some reason I recalled another old border ballad, 'The Dowie Dens o' Yarrow':

As he gaed up yon high, high hills,
Doon by the braes o' Yarrow,
It was there he saw nine armed men,
Come tae fecht wi' him on Yarrow.
And three he slew and three they flew,
And three he wounded sairly,
Till her brither John came in beyond,
And did murder him maist foully.

It seems that the banks of Yarrow might be best avoided, and neighbouring Yair, in our experience, is nowhere to linger either. After stopping for a quick lunch (we were now looking forward to fish and chips later in the afternoon), we dropped down to Yair and a number of big, expensive-looking houses. No sooner had we hit the road than a Subaru estate car came screaming around the corner, and further on a sign proclaimed the welcome, 'Any cars parked on this estate will be clamped.' I was glad we were leaving.

MUCH OF THIS ROUTE FOLLOWS THE LINE OF THE SOUTHERN UPLAND WAY

•

Over the Tweed by its old bridge, up the long and steep road out of Fairnilee Farm and over Hogg Hill for our last stretch until we reached Galashiels. Just past the little house at Calfshaw we met a group of 25 ramblers, a coterie of multicoloured fleece jackets and bobble hats marching along, not one of them appearing to be under 60 years of age, and they sounded as if they were having a whale of a time.

Down through the woods into Galashiels now and into the town just past the school close to where the Gala Water runs into the mighty Tweed.

Out ower yon moss, out ower yon muir,
Out ower yon bonnie bush o' heather
O a' ye lads whae'er ye be,
Show me the way to Gala Water,
Braw, braw bonnie lads o'.

Despite the wonderful ballad, Galashiels is not a particularly inspiring place at which to end a walk. Finishing a walk in a town is always faintly depressing – the contrast between high, open countryside and urban sprawl can be disturbing – as doing so breaks the sense of the mysterious interrelatedness of everything, where all are one, rocks, trees and beasts, the living and the dead. Some would say that this is a rather tribal notion, a primeval way of seeing the world, but there is a sense that, although the world is a sacred place and full of wonder, the wild places give a feeling of intimacy, of belonging.

It was good to find the car, our thoughts full of the delights of our walk – Ettrick and Scabcleuch, Riskinhope Hope and Blake Muir, and to a lesser extent the high level walk in the footsteps of kings and drovers over Minch Moor. I can now understand something of the attraction of the Borders and why so many people would want to write songs about it. We went with a song in our hearts, a new-found song of the Borders, its rolling hills, its history and its fusion of time, ballad and story. Bruce Chatwin had a vision of the Songlines stretching across the continents and ages, that wherever men have trodden they have left a trail of song, of which we may, now and then, catch an echo. Man has left a wonderful trail of song in the Scottish Borders, and its echoes still ring out through the ages, to those who will listen.

CHAPTER TWO

GALLOWAY

STRESS RELIEF ON THE RANGE OF THE AWFUL HAND

•

Cameron McNeish

A three-day walk around the tops of the Galloway Forest Park, from Loch Trool to the Rhinns of Kells, Loch Enoch and the Merrick

---

MAP: *Harvey's 1:25 000 Galloway Hills, OS 1:50 000 Sheet 77*
START AND FINISH: *Bruce's Stone car park, Glen Trool. Grid Ref: 416803*
LENGTH: *25 miles (40 km)*
APPROXIMATE TIME: *3 days*
TERRAIN: *Some track on the Southern Upland Way but predominantly trackless mountain-walking over some of the roughest terrain I've experienced in Scotland*
ACCOMMODATION: *A campsite at Caldons in Glen Trool, where there is also a shop that sells sweets, food, drinks and maps. Glen Trool Visitor Centre also has a café and small shop open from Easter to the end of October. Hotels, guest-houses and b&bs in Newton Stewart (about 13 miles/20 km from Loch Trool) and youth hostels at Minigaff, Newton Stewart and Kendoon, near Dalry*

I felt curiously unhappy. The weekend stretched before me, I was going to explore new hills and glens in an area that I'd wanted to visit for years, and I was setting off to do the very thing that I enjoy more than anything else; yet for tuppence I would have turned my back on it all, jumped into my car and driven home.

I was emotionally torn, with a monkey on my back whispering negatives in my ear. I knew I had left a lot of work at home, various domestic matters required my attention, and I was only too well aware that the weather forecast wasn't great. I didn't need reminding. And yet at the same time I was edgy and desperate to get going, hurrying myself along, fumbling over my bootlaces and gaiters, undecided as to whether I should take my camera or not. I felt irritable, and a tension at the base of my skull suggested the beginnings of a headache.

Eventually, I heaved the pack on my back, locked the car and began walking with a

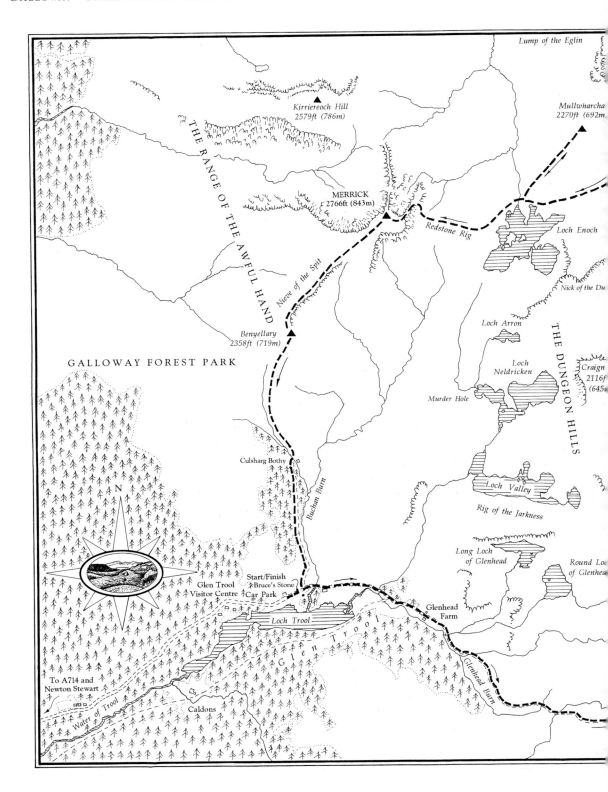

Lump of the Eglin

Kirriereoch Hill 2579ft (786m)

Mullwharcha 2270ft (692m)

THE RANGE OF THE AWFUL HAND

MERRICK 2766ft (843m)

Redstone Rig

Loch Enoch

Nieve of the Spit

Nick of the Du

Benyellary 2358ft (719m)

Loch Arron

GALLOWAY FOREST PARK

Loch Neldricken

Craign 2116f (645

THE DUNGEON HILLS

Murder Hole

N

Culsharg Bothy

Buchan Burn

Loch Valley

Rig of the Jarkness

Long Loch of Glenhead

Round Lo of Glenhea

Glen Trool Visitor Centre

Start/Finish Bruce's Stone Car Park

Glenhead Farm

Loch Trool

Glen Trool

Glenhead Burn

To A714 and Newton Stewart

Water of Trool

Caldons

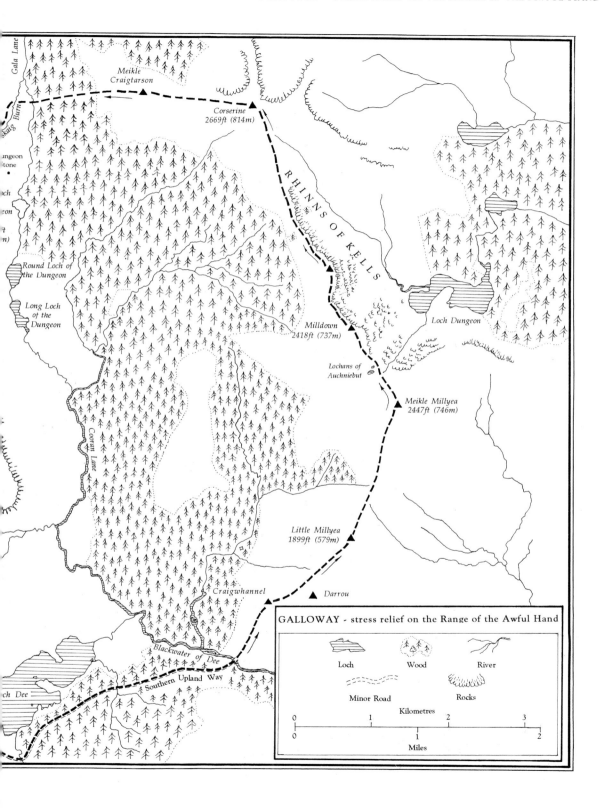

Gala Lane

Meikle
Craigtarson

Corserine
2669ft (814m)

R H I N S   O F   K E L L S

ungeon
tone

ch
eon

t
n)

Round Loch of
the Dungeon

Long Loch
of the
Dungeon

Milldown
2418ft (737m)

Loch Dungeon

Lochans of
Auchniebut

Cooran Lane

Meikle Millyea
2447ft (746m)

Little Millyea
1899ft (579m)

Craigwhannel

Darrou

Blackwater of Dee

ch Dee

Southern Upland Way

GALLOWAY - stress relief on the Range of the Awful Hand

Loch   Wood   River

Minor Road   Rocks

Kilometres

0   1   2   3

0   1   2

Miles

purposeful stride. It was the weekend of the spring equinox and within half an hour it would be dark, but I hadn't gone more than half a mile before the monkey started chattering again. He convinced me that I had left my reading glasses in the car. One of the joys of backpacking is that I get a rare opportunity to indulge myself in a good book, and without my specs I couldn't read, so I took off my pack and checked. They were there, safely tucked away in the lid pocket.

A few hundred yards further on the blasted monkey was jumping up and down again. Where had I put my lighter? Without it I wouldn't be able to light my stove. Pack off again and I checked it out: there it was, neatly stowed away inside the stove bag.

By this time I was concerned. I've been at this backpacking game for more years than I remember, yet here I was fretting like a tyro. Worried about leaving my car in the car park, worried in case I lost my car keys, worried about relatively unimportant domestic matters… It was when I began to fret about the week that was just over that I knew immediately what was wrong with me. I was stressed. Not suicidally stressed, and not even clinically stressed, but uptight enough to make little problems appear leviathan. And in tandem with that sudden realization came the comforting knowledge that I was doing the right thing.

Large portions of our lives tend to be governed by problems and schedules imposed on us by other people. Pressures are created, sometimes resulting in intolerable levels of stress. Walking through wilderness offers an escape from that. We can walk where we want to. We can go fast or slow, hard or easy. We can go by ourselves or with friends. We can think great thoughts or simply empty our minds. The vital thing is that the choice is ours – no one makes the decisions for us, and furthermore we can change them according to the minute-by-minute requirements and fancies of our minds and bodies. On top of that, research has shown that exercise not only stimulates our blood vessels and denser nerve connections but actually pumps more blood to the brain, with the effect that the simple act of walking can help keep our brain in better shape. That means we are better able to deal with the myriad complexities of life which, for many of us, can so often result in unacceptable high levels of stress.

I had left my car in the parking area near the head of Glen Trool, a lovely spot in the heart of Galloway. The nearby Bruce's Stone monument celebrates a clash with English forces in 1307 when Robert the Bruce was just beginning his campaign for the Scottish throne. This was an area he knew well, and the broken hillsides and scattered woodland of Glen Trool was ideal for his style of guerrilla warfare. This same landscape, despite the incursions of dense conifer plantations, now draws tourists by the carload, most of whom don't leave the pretty confines of the glen. My intention was to walk for a couple of miles and camp for the night, and then, on the following day, to follow the route of the Southern Upland Way past Loch Dee to the Blackwater of Dee, from where I would follow the long ridge of the Rhinns of Kells to its northern summit of Corserine, the second highest of these Galloway hills. On the third day I wanted to climb Mullwharchar and the Merrick before returning to my car at Bruce's Stone car park. I was worrying about the descent from Corserine, through what looked on the map like impenetrable forest, when I walked into an exceedingly muddy farmyard. I'd missed a turning in the footpath.

A great billy goat stared at me disconsolately, chickens screeched and a mêlée of dogs started up a hideous din from an adjoining barn. I expected all the lights in the farmhouse to suddenly come on and a voice shout: 'Who's there?' But the house stayed dark, despite the cacophony from the farm animals. Pack off once again, I dug out the map and shone my headtorch on it. It was obvious that I had missed a turning and had walked into Glenhead farm. No real harm done – the turning was only a couple of hundred yards back – but it was enough to give me a jolt. It was almost dark now, and I needed to pay more attention.

On the correct route, I followed the footpath across Glenhead Burn and followed its southern bank in the growing darkness. Once the path left the riverside and started climbing up into the pitch-black forest, I decided it was time to look for a camp. The narrow path soon converged onto a broad forest drive, adjacent to which was a flat stony patch of ground. This would do for my first night.

Tent up, cosily ensconced in my sleeping-bag and a mug of tea in hand, the tensions began to evaporate. The simplicity of backpacking, walking and camping in wild places has been a way of life for nomadic tribes for thousands of years. The backpacker, like the early caveman, reverts to a hunter-gatherer status, and life becomes simple again. Like us, those early ancestors were equipped with a gland-like hypothalamus, situated at the base of the brain, which, in certain situations, secreted hormones that would prepare the body for a state of high alert. Heart rate and breathing would speed up, blood pressure would be raised, and adrenaline would begin to flow; the body was then prepared to fight the sabre-toothed tiger or run away from it.

Although our brains have evolved and have become bigger, and our thinking processes are probably much more complex than those of early man, this fight-or-flight response is still part and parcel of the nervous system. Have you ever had butterflies in your stomach at the thought of danger? Ever heard your heart pounding? Do you suffer from a stiff back or stiff neck after a stressful meeting? These physical characteristics are all symptoms of our autonomic nervous system, preparing our body, and mind, for fight or flight. But our modern stressors tend to be less obvious than a straightforward confrontation with a sabre-toothed tiger. Bosses, tax inspections, examinations and budgets are not directly life threatening, but sometimes we react to them as if they were, and, while situations trigger our stress responses, outlets for the extra hormones and chemicals produced by our bodies are rare. The effect of these extra hormones can result in physical and psychological problems like depression, anxiety, sleeplessness and mood swings – we have a Stone Age psychology that is trying to adapt to a modern way of life. And that is the problem. The simplest answer is to go wild.

Glenhead to Gala Lane

•

Morning dawned windy and grey, but at least the rain that had fallen in the night had cleared. I felt much better than I had the night before, and I was eager to get going. A good night's sleep, despite the gusty wind, had made all the difference, and the smell of pines and humus filling my nostrils began to work its healing power. It was, after all, good to be here.

There's something otherworldly about Galloway's hills. The tops stand aloof, like islands, from the serried waves of forestry plantations, and the placenames evoke hobgoblin plots of doom and disaster: Dungeon Hill, the Range of the Awful Hand, the Murder Hole, The Wolf Slock… There's a Tolkienesque mind-set at work here: Mullwharchar, Craigwhannel and Craigmasheenie, Rig of the Jarkness, Curleywee, Lump of the Eglin, Shalloch on Minnoch and Cairnsmore of Carsphairn. I know of no other area in Scotland that can boast such extraordinary placenames.

For the first couple of hours the going was easy, along a broad forest road following the little acorn symbols of the Southern Upland Way, past the southern shores of Loch Dee and over the bridge on the Blackwater of Dee. Low cloud obscured most of the views as I tried desperately to relate my position with where I would be going. There was a lot of conifer forest hereabouts which reminded me that I could have difficulties coming off the Rhinns of Kells through the dense forest, but that wouldn't be until later in the afternoon. For the moment I could hang that particular problem to one side and concentrate on the problem at hand. I had to climb onto the butt-end of the long ridge of the Rhinns of Kells, and that looked as though it would be a real sweat.

I was right: it *was* a sweat, but not as hard as I expected. A forest ride, above a small quarry, gave access to the start of the Rhinns of Kells, a small hummocky hill with a great granite erratic gracing its summit. This was Craigwhannel, just over 1312 feet (400 m) above sea-level but densely shrouded in the mist. I took a straight compass bearing for Little Millyea, bypassing the second top of the ridge, the curiously named Darrou, but it didn't take long before I realized that this traverse of the Rhinns of Kells wasn't going to be as straightforward as I'd imagined. The ground was wet and boggy and the bleached yellow grasses grew up into high tussocks. This rough terrain had the potential to break ankles, and tempers. So much for stress relief!

According to the Scottish author and mountaineer Hamish Brown, the name Millyea is a corruption of the Gaelic Meall Liath, or 'grey rounded hill'. It's a long,

PREVIOUS PAGES: LOVELY GLEN TROOL FROM CRAIGNAW HILL, A GREEN OASIS AMID THE RUGGED GRANDEUR OF GALLOWAY FOREST PARK

•

long time since Gaelic was spoken in Galloway, and it could be that throughout those centuries the evolution of placenames has led to some of the weird and wonderful names that exist here today. Shortly after Little Millyea, a stone wall wound a sinuous line uphill to Meikle Millyea and then across a watery col (past the Lochans of Auchniebut) to the flat-topped Milldown. Here the wind was incessant and seemed to be gaining in strength. Every now and again it would blow away the cloud, and I'd be greeted with superb mountainous views beyond a great sea of conifer plantation before the mist swept in once more, obscuring everything in its grey shroud-like curtain.

This conifer-tide flows high on the western flanks of the Rhinns of Kells, but beyond the trees the dramatically named Dungeon Hills looked absolutely superb. There are some captivating names here: the Round Loch of the Dungeon, the Long Loch of the Dungeon…there is a Dungeon Stone, Dungeon Hill and a neighbouring top with the unlikely name of Nick of the Dungeon. And to balance things up, away below me on the eastern side of the Kells ridge lay Loch Dungeon. North of the Dungeon Hills lay another odd-sounding hill, a curious name in a land of curious names. Mullwharchar is also apparently derived from the Gaelic Maol Adhairce, meaning 'hill of the huntsman's horn', and I wanted to camp below it tonight.

Up here, tramping up the final slopes of Corserine, the second-highest hill in Galloway and a Corbett (a Scottish hill between 2500 and 2999.9 feet/762 and 914 m), the wind had reached gale-force proportions, but despite that, and the cold nipping my fingers, I felt relaxed. Indeed, I was enjoying myself even though my legs felt heavy and I guessed I wasn't as fit as I should have been. The stress antidote was working.

As I struggled into the wind, the westward descent from Corserine almost caught me unawares. I was now walking into the very teeth of the westerly gale, and the wind pulled and pushed at me like an all-in wrestler. Despite my trying to follow a compass bearing the wind constantly blew me off course. Only frequent references to my map and compass kept me on the right line. It wasn't until I began dropping down the steep slopes of Corserine's outlier, Meikle Craigtarson, that I could relax. Earlier I had been concerned with how I was going to get through the thick band of seemingly impenetrable forest that lay between me and the infant Gala Lane burn where I wanted to camp, but in practice the eventual route couldn't have been simpler. A forest ride cut right through the trees, complete, as it happened, with a well-worn if boggy footpath. The deer, sheep and goats obviously appreciated the route through the forest too. I guessed it was they who had made the path, rather than the tread of human feet.

A camp, protected by the trees from the wind and close to the Gala Lane burn, was my treat, and it was a tired walker who collapsed into his tent to review what had been a fairly hard but satisfying 14-mile (22-km) day – simply myself against the hill, the tussocky ground and the wind. My navigation in the cloud and mist had been faultless, and I reckoned another day of the same and I'd be ready to join the human race again.

Above: The granite basin that holds the waters of Loch Enoch surrounded on three sides by high, rugged hills

Right: Loch Dee and the distant Rhinns of Kells

Mullwharchar to Glen Trool

•

Morning dawned dank and misty, the cloud down to valley level. It had rained fairly gently during the night but all in all it had been a peaceful night. Well aware that it looked like being another map and compass day, I was anxious to get going fairly early.

The route now climbed, up the narrowing glen of Pulskaig Burn, the silver waters of the stream chuckling over its slabby Galloway granite bed, to the big rocky bowl that holds the waters of Loch Enoch. From there I wanted to climb the oddly named Mullwharchar, and then climb the Merrick by its easterly Redstone Rig.

Within five minutes of leaving I knew it was going to be another hard day. Deep tussocks made the going extremely unstable, and where the ground wasn't tussocky it was boggy. I followed a rough goats' track up the southern bank of the burn, enjoying its chattering company. The cloud lay like a shroud, but there was little sign of the wind of yesterday. It was hard work, but I didn't mind. I knew the effort was worth it and I would reap the benefits in more ways than one.

Dr Hans Selye, author of *Stress Without Distress,* has been studying stress for decades. One way to help avoid undue suffering from the effects of stress is to exercise our body. 'Often,' Dr Selye writes, 'a voluntary change of activity is as good as or even better than rest. For example, when either fatigue or enforced interruption prevents us from finishing a mathematical problem, it is better to go for a swim (or a walk) than simply to sit around. Substituting demands on our muscles for those previously made on the intellect not only gives our brain a rest but helps us avoid worrying about the other.'

Substituting stressors can have much the same effect. Although I was no longer worrying about the problems of the week just past, I would be lying if I suggested I was floating on heavenly clouds. I was working damned hard, I was concentrating on navigational problems in the mist, and I was taking care not to twist an ankle on the difficult terrain. I knew that such an accident could have dire consequences in a place like this, so life was hardly stress free – the stressors were just different. What better way could there be to substitute physical exercise for mental exercise than to walk in wild places, where the beauty around you acts as a stimulus and the natural peace stills your soul?

Soon the climb began to level out, and I took a compass bearing, intent on finding the northern shores of Loch Enoch. I was in strange country, with bluffs and granite pavements scattered on the tussocky moorland. Boulders lay everywhere, scattered around at random after being swept along by glaciers aeons ago. I couldn't see more than about 100 feet (30 m) in front of me, but the high-pitched calls of young feral goats sounded like the cries of children, the children of the mists. It was an eerie sound. Not long after I came across the depression that held the grey waters of Loch Enoch, and almost at the same time something magical happened: as I stood still, the cloud suddenly shifted, like a curtain dragged aside, to expose the loch and, beyond, the rugged slopes of the Merrick, its rounded profile looking benign and friendly in the fresh light. And no sooner had the cloud shifted than the air was full of the song of skylarks, an outpouring of such joy and vigour that I felt like crying out myself.

Only now could I really appreciate the wild surroundings of this, the very heart of Galloway. The waters of Loch Enoch lie in a high granite basin that caresses the 1600-foot (491-m) contour line, and the ragged shorelines are surrounded on three sides by high hills: Dungeon Hill, Mullwharchar and the Merrick. To its south the land falls away in a series of craggy terraces, each terrace holding another loch: Loch Arron, Loch Neldricken and Loch Valley. Beyond them lie Long Loch of Glenhead and Round Loch of Glenhead, a real rosary of lakes. It's said that the silver sand of Loch Enoch's beaches was once collected for sharpening knives.

Beyond the south-west shores of Loch Enoch the long line of Redstone Rig could be seen rising steadily to the Merrick's summit, but before I tackled Redstone Rig I wanted to backtrack a little and climb Mullwharchar – a climb of only some 650 feet (200 m) or so, but I wished to visit the 2270-foot (692-m) summit, where geologists had wanted to drill the hard granite rock a few years ago to test its suitability for the disposal of nuclear waste from Windscale, just across the Solway Firth. So far nothing has come of this proposal, but I wanted to familiarize myself with the mountain in preparation for a genuine fight-or-flight response should the suggestion be raised again.

Now that the cloud had cleared I looked forward to good views from the Merrick's summit – I had heard tales of views of the English Lake District to the Mourne Mountains of Ulster, the Arran Peaks and even Ben Lomond. Although I had a fairly good localized view from Mullwharchar, with drifting cloud obscuring all but the neighbouring hills, I saw only the trig point and wind shelter on the summit of the Merrick. As soon as I had set foot on the rough slopes of Redstone Rig the cloud returned with a vengeance and all hopes of a view were dashed. Despite that, I felt curiously exultant. The high rounded bulk of the Merrick dominates the hills around Loch Trool, and this 'branched finger' is the highest in the Range of the Awful Hand. Indeed at 2766 feet (843 m) it's the highest summit in the Galloway Hills. I know I had a fairly easy ridge walk and descent in front of me and that the hard work was now over. This Galloway wasn't easy country. It didn't give up its secrets mildly, and I knew that I would have to come back again to enjoy the wider aspects of its far-flung views. Despite my euphoria, the descent felt like a long one, across the narrow Nieve of the Spit to neighbouring Benyellary, a bastardization of Beinn na h-Iolaire, 'hill of the eagle', and a muddy trot down the well-worn footpath into the forest, past what is left of Culsharg Bothy and down a dreadfully eroded track back to Bruce's Stone. I had seen no one for a couple of days but now the forest trail was busy with families enjoying a day out. I didn't grudge them it. Indeed, increasing numbers of people are recognizing and embracing a pretty fundamental credo that I've been fortunate enough to know for a long time: to misquote Henry David Thoreau, in wilderness is the preservation of the *mind*.

MULLWHARCHAR, A PROPOSED SITE FOR THE DUMPING OF NUCLEAR WASTE

•

CHAPTER THREE

AROUND THE TROSSACHS

FOLLOWING THE FIERY CROSS

•

Cameron McNeish

A three-day walk around the Trossachs area of the southern Highlands, following in the footsteps of the heroes of Sir Walter Scott

---

MAPS: *OS 1:50 000 Sheets 56 and 57*
START AND FINISH: *The pier at Loch Katrine. Grid Ref: 495072*
LENGTH: *55 miles (88 km)*
APPROXIMATE TIME: *3 days*
TERRAIN: *A mixture of rough mountain slopes and a variety of footpaths*
ACCOMMODATION: *A hotel at the foot of Ben An and b&bs at Brig o' Turk. Hotels, guest-houses and b&bs at Callander and Strathyre and a few b&bs at Balquhidder*

The word 'Trossachs' is derived from 'Trosaichen', a word now obsolete in the Gaelic language meaning a transverse glen joining two others. It's a description that loosely fits the heartland of the Trossachs area, the great tumble of rock and trees which separates Loch Katrine from Loch Achray. Loch Katrine is a reservoir supplying water to the Glasgow metropolis, and a steamer, appropriately named *Sir Walter Scott*, plies the loch with day-trippers during the summer. As I shouldered my pack on a quiet and misty morning, there was every promise of a great day ahead.

The road from the car park runs for about a mile to its junction with the A821 Aberfoyle to Callander road, a particularly beautiful stretch through a wooded gorge formed between Ben Venue in the south and rocky Ben An in the north. The green buds of oak, larch and birch filtered the faint sunlight, and great beams pierced the mist like pale green spotlights.

Ben An was my first destination, and I relished the thought of sitting up there on its rocky crest soaking up a view that is often considered to be one of the finest in

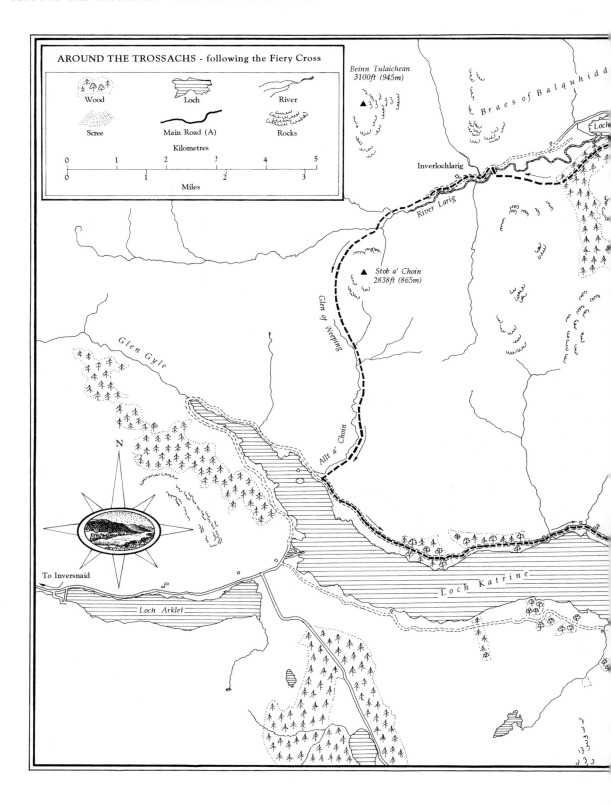

AROUND THE TROSSACHS - following the Fiery Cross

Wood

Loch

River

Scree

Main Road (A)

Rocks

Kilometres

0 1 2 3 4 5

0 1 2 3

Miles

Beinn Tulaichean
3100ft (945m)

Braes of Balquhidd

Loch

Inverlochlarig

River Larig

Stob a' Choin
2838ft (865m)

Glen of Weeping

Glen Gyle

N

Allt a' Choin

To Inversnaid

Loch Arklet

Loch Katrine

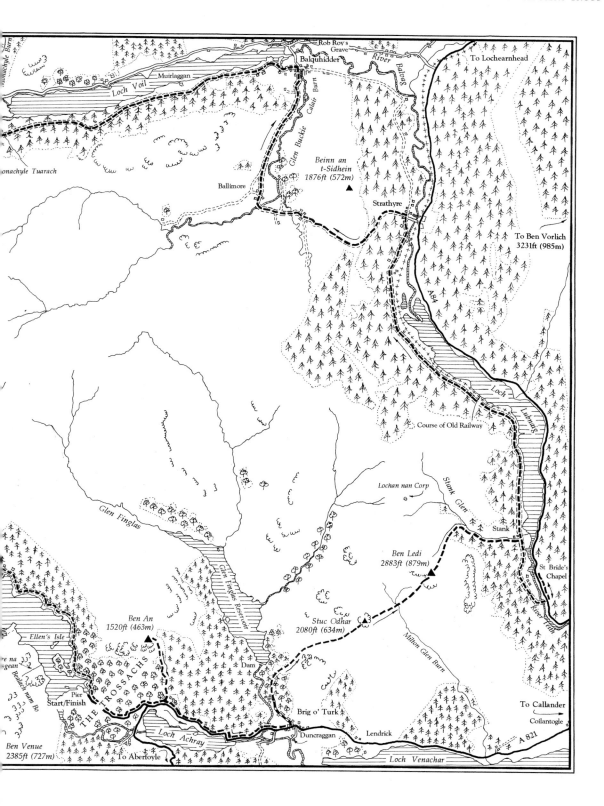

Onachyle Tuarach

Loch Voil

Muirlaggan

Balquhidder

Rob Roy's Grave

River Balvag

To Lochearnhead

Glen Buckie

Calair Burn

Beinn an
t-Sidhein
1876ft (572m)

Ballimore

Strathyre

To Ben Vorlich
3231ft (985m)

A84

Loch Lubnaig

Course of Old Railway

Glen Finglas

Lochan nan Corp

Stank Glen

Stank

Ben Ledi
2883ft (879m)

St Bride's
Chapel

Ben An
1520ft (463m)

Glen Finglas Reservoir

Stuc Odhar
2080ft (634m)

Ellen's Isle

Milton Glen Burn

River Teith

re na
sgean

Bealach nam Bo

Pier
Start/Finish

THE TROSSACHS

Dam

Brig o' Turk

Lendrick

To Callander

Coilantogle

Ben Venue
2385ft (727m)

To Aberfoyle

Loch Achray

Duncraggan

Loch Venachar

A 821

southern Scotland. A signpost indicated the path which leads up through the trees to Ben An, a mere 1520 feet (463 m) above sea-level, but a rocky spire of tremendous character, offering more in its meagre height than many hills of twice its size.

On top I enjoyed the warmth of the morning sun, and the mist was rapidly burning off around me. Ben Venue, across the gorge of the Trossachs, stood out against a deep blue sky, and the summit slopes of the Crianlarich and Arrochar hills to the west stood out like islands on a white ocean.

Ben An isn't the original name of this hill. The old Gaelic name was Am Binnein, 'the rocky peak', but that was changed, like some other local names, to suit the poetic licence of Sir Walter Scott. Scott has had a considerable influence on this area. Some say he was the instigator of Highland tourism, and he was directly responsible for this trip that I had just set out on.

This Trossachs area sits on the very edge of the Highland Line, a geological and geographical fault which runs across Scotland from the southern end of Loch Lomond to Stonehaven on the north-east coast. The clans who inhabited the regions north of this line were, even until a couple of hundred years ago, virtually sequestered from the civilized world. Living under an ancient clan system, they tended to live by their own rules and laws and by a patriarchal system which went back centuries.

Ever since reading *The Lady of the Lake* and *Rob Roy*, I had been enthralled by the history of the Trossachs area, and in particular by the doings of the Gregorach, the Clan Macgregor. Their erstwhile chief, Rob Roy Macgregor Campbell, like the area he ruled, owes much of his fame to Scott, who painted a rather colourful picture of this Scottish Robin Hood. Rob Roy became chief of the Macgregors through sheer personality rather than by virtue of descent and, although a rogue and scoundrel of the first order, he had a cheeky, albeit clever manner that endeared him to the common folk. My favourite tale concerning Rob is of an incident in the year 1716, when, on his way from Inversnaid on Loch Lomond to Aberfoyle, he was approached by a clansman with a sad tale to relate. A poor widow, a Macgregor, a tenant on the Duke of Montrose's estate, had fallen into arrears with her rent, and that very day everything she owned was to be sold by the duke's factor to make up the debt. Rob immediately called on the widow and advanced her the sum that was due, telling her that when the factor arrived she was to give him the money and make certain that she obtained a receipt for it. Not far from the widow's cottage was an inn at which the duke's factor invariably stopped for refreshment whenever he was in the area. When he arrived, after collecting the money from the widow, he was confronted by the Macgregor and several of his men. Firmly but politely, they relieved him of all the money in his possession. Rob Roy was no longer out of pocket, and the widow had a receipt to prove that she had paid her annual rent. Such was the style of Rob Roy Macgregor.

Born on 7 March 1671 in a little house at Glengyle, near the head of Loch Katrine, Rob Roy was the son of Lieutenant-Colonel Donald Macgregor, an officer in the army

ABOVE: LOCH KATRINE FROM
THE SUMMIT OF BEN AN

LEFT: LOCH LUBNAIG FROM
BEINN AN T-SIDHEIN, THE HILL
OF THE FAIRIES

•

of Charles II, and Margaret Campbell. She was half-sister to the later despised Campbell of Glenlyon, who was responsible for carrying out the evil deeds at the Massacre of Glencoe in 1692, when a band of government soldiers turned on their hosts, the Macdonalds of Glencoe, and murdered them in the night, desecrating the Highland tradition of hospitality. As the name Macgregor was at that time proscribed, the minister refused to baptize the baby, and Donald had to carry the young Rob to the adjoining parish of Buchanan. This proscription, or banning, of the name Macgregor occurred after a particularly vicious clan battle with the Colquhouns of Luss. The Macgregors had always been a pretty volatile crew but were in many ways no worse than other Highland clans. Feuding, stealing and cattle-reiving had been a way of life in the Highlands for centuries, but in 1593 James IV of Scotland became determined to reduce the chaos of the Highlands to some sort of law and order. He introduced an act known as the General Band, or Bond. If any clansman were accused of a crime, his landlord must produce him to answer the charge, or pay the damages himself. The chiefs found themselves paying through the nose for the actions of their clansfolk. Alasdair of Glenstrae, the Macgregor chief at the time, appeared himself before the court and promised that his people would behave in a lawful manner, a rather rash promise, for despite his promise the reivings and raidings inevitably went on.

Once proscribed, the Macgregors had to change their name. Worse was to come: anyone, according to a new law, was at liberty to kill a Macgregor on sight and claim his goods and lands. Any known criminal or murderer would receive a pardon if he could produce a Macgregor, dead or alive. The law applied to all the male members of the clan over the age of 14. The women were not forgotten, though: if they were known to be Macgregors they were to be branded on the face and transported, and their children left behind to fend for themselves.

The Gregorach took to the hills, hiding in caves and hollows. They slept by day and flitted like shadows into the glens at night to steal food for their families. These nocturnal doings soon earned them the name Children of the Mist, and the name Macgregor became one that struck fear and dread into the hearts of law-abiding citizens, whether Highlander or Lowlander.

This new-found notoriety was used to advantage by some of the smarter Macgregors. For an annual fee, bands of men protected the cattle of the rich merchants and farmers who lived on the borders of the Highland Line. Soon, this protection racket became big business and was even later approved by the government, no doubt delighted to see the rebels settle down as prosperous businessmen. These Watches, as they were known, were set up throughout the Highlands, and Rob Roy's father became joint Captain of the Highland Watch. (The Watches were later turned into armed forces – hence the birth of the Black Watch Regiment.) Rob's father, particularly infamous for his 'lifting' exploits, died in 1693, so the responsibility of the clan chieftaincy, and the captaincy of the Highland Watch, fell on Rob's shoulders.

Rob was not actually in the line of descent for such titles, being only the second son, but such was his influence over his elder brother John, even at the age of 22, that his brother declined the responsibilities in favour of Rob.

Rob Roy ran his Highland Watch in a shrewd businesslike manner, and woe betide anyone who was late with his dues, whether he was the local minister, or the Lord Justice Clerk. Rob Roy was no great respecter of persons.

The Trossachs area that now lay around me in the morning sunshine was Macgregor country, a rough and tumbled land that was used to advantage by the clan throughout the centuries. The route that I had come to follow was that course taken by the bearers of the Fiery Cross, or Crean Tarigh, the Cross of Shame. When a chieftain desired to summon his clan, he slew a goat and, making a cross of any light wood, seared the ends of the cross in a fire, then extinguished the flames in the blood of the slain animal. The cross was then carried around the clan lands by a relay of runners, who passed the cross to each other with a single word – the place of rendezvous. At the sight of the Fiery Cross, every man from age 16 to 60 and capable of bearing arms was obliged to present himself instantly at the given rendezvous. Any who failed to appear suffered the extreme punishments of fire and sword, which were emblematically demonstrated to the disobedient by the bloody and burnt marks of the cross.

In Scott's *The Lady of the Lake*, the cross was carried from 'Lanric Mead', nowadays known as Lendrick, at the western end of Loch Venachar, one of the lochs now shimmering below me. This was the traditional assembly point for the Gregorach, and it was near here, at Duncraggan, that Angus, heir of 'Duncan's line', was summoned to carry the first stage of the Fiery Cross. According to Scott, Angus sped quickly along the shores of Loch Venachar to Coilantogle, where he ascended the broad ridge of Ben Ledi and dropped down steeply to the Pass of Leny.

A road nowadays runs alongside Loch Venachar to Coilantogle, and since I was anxious to avoid as much road-walking as possible I decided to skirt a little of the original Fiery Cross route and to take a short cut, although it was rougher country, over the summit of Ben Ledi.

I turned off the main road at Brig o' Turk to take the very minor road to Glen Finglas Dam. Brig o' Turk is an odd-sounding name for a Highland village and is derived from the Gaelic word 'tuirc' meaning 'wild boar'. In the days of Rob Roy, Brig o' Turk was a hamlet inhabited by wild drovers, and it had the reputation of being a pretty dangerous place. Today it couldn't look tamer, and one or two faces peeped from behind closed curtains as I stomped past, no doubt wondering who could be disturbing their peace at such an early hour, and outside the tourist season too!

OVERLEAF: LOCH VOIL AND THE SNOW-CLAD BRAES O' BALQUHIDDER

•

Glen Finglas, a fine glen between Ben An and Ben Ledi, is well and truly flooded by the waters of the Glen Finglas Reservoir. To the east rose the long, broken slopes of Ben Ledi; it is a good two miles (three km) to the summit of Ledi from Glen Finglas, with almost 2000 feet (610 m) of climbing, but the going is easy over tufted grass and short heather.

An old fence runs over the subsidiary top of Stuc Odhar and down to the bealach that gives birth to Milton Glen Burn. On the opposite side of the bealach rise the final slopes of Ben Ledi. Rather than follow a direct line up the steep slopes to the summit, I traversed a little northwards and climbed the gentler north-west ridge by way of some pleasant grassy gullies. As I reached the summit ridge, the white trig point stood out like a beacon against the dark blue of the sky. The view was superb: all of the south, from the flats of Flanders Moss to as far as the eye could see, was covered by an ocean of cloud, with only the high tops of the Campsie Fells piercing the whiteness; to the north-east, Ben Vorlich was hidden by its close neighbour, Stuc a' Chroin, and beyond them the great Lawers massif stood out clearly, white-fringed with snow against the blue; below me, Loch Lubnaig and the Pass of Leny were barely discernible through a gossamer-thin film of mist.

I made my way along to the trig point and cairn. The exact derivation of the name is 'Ben le Dia', the 'Hill of God'. Flat stretches of turf on the summit ridge have been associated with the Beltane, or May Day Festival, which used to be held here annually. The ceremonies that took place were thought to be a version of a druidic ceremony involving a human sacrifice to the sun-god Baal, although no stones or artefacts have been found to substantiate this theory. To heighten further the somewhat grisly aspect of the mountain's history, a small lochan lies about a mile north of the summit. This is Lochan nan Corp, or 'the small loch of the dead bodies'. Centuries ago, in the depths of winter, a cortege of mourners was following an old coffin route across the hill from Glen Finglas to St Bride's Chapel in the Pass of Leny. As they crossed the frozen waters of the lochan, the ice cracked open and several of the mourners drowned in the bitterly cold water.

My descent route led down to Stank Glen, past a weird and fantastic jumble of rock outcrops, broken clawing shapes some 50 feet (15 m) or so in height, towering above me like malevolent fingers pointing out the road to Hades!

I had walked about ten miles (sixteen km) since leaving Loch Katrine, and it was now early afternoon. The village of Strathyre, with its pleasant little campsite, was still some way distant, but first I wanted to visit the remains of St Bride's Chapel, so I pressed on down through the forest trail of Stank Glen. It was pleasant to walk in the shade for a while, and the pungent smell of the sun-warmed pine clung to my notrils. The path was richly carpeted in pine needles, and walking on such a pleasant surface was a relief after the knee-jarring descent through the rocks and screes above. How different it was for Sir Walter Scott's hero Angus as he fled down the hill with the dreadful symbol of war clutched firmly in his grasp. All indications in the poem show that the weather was probably foul; mention is made of mountain breezes and, to make matters worse, when he reached the foot of Ledi to hand the cross over to the next bearer, he found the River Teith in spate:

> Swoln was the stream, remote the bridge,
> But Angus paused not on the edge,
> Though the dark waves danced dizzily,
> Though reeled his sympathetic eye,
> He dashed amidst the torrent's roar,
> His right hand the crosslet bore,
> His left the pole axe grasped to guide,
> And stay his footing on the tide.

My crossing wasn't quite so dramatic. The ruins lie on the eastern bank of the River Teith, beside the busy A84 Callander to Lochearnhead road, and it was hard to imagine bygone scenes. As Angus, dripping wet, staggered up the pathway to the church, a wedding was in progress. Unfortunately, the next bearer in the relay of the cross was one Norman, heir of Armandave, the bridegroom! As he escorted his blushing bride from the chapel, little could he have thought what was in store.

> With virgin step, and bashful hand,
> She held the kerchief's snowy band,
> The gallant bridegroom by her side,
> Beheld his prize with Victor's pride,
> And the glad mother in her ear,
> Was closely whispering words of cheer,
> But, who meets them at the churchyard gate?

Who indeed? Brave Angus, sodden wet from his river crossing! And so poor Norman bade farewell to his new wife and set off, cross in hand, towards Strathyre.

From Stank, an old railway cutting hugs the western shore of Loch Lubnaig, providing a first-class track for walkers. Some oystercatchers cried noisily overhead, and a pair of madcap lapwings cavorted crazily, diving and soaring in their deranged mating game. The village of Strathyre, the 'Bonnie Strathyre' of the song of the same name, sits comfortably at the head of Loch Lubnaig. In the days of Rob Roy and co. the village was known as Nineveh because of the number of public houses it boasted. Nearby Balquhidder was even better, boasting no fewer than six pubs! I stopped in the campsite just outside the village and in the name of research felt obliged to sample at least one of the remaining pubs of Strathyre.

ABOVE: BALQUHIDDER KIRK, THE FINAL
RESTING PLACE OF ROB ROY

RIGHT: LOOKING WEST DOWN THE
LENGTH OF LOCH VOIL

•

Strathyre to the Glen of Weeping
•

Directly west of the village, across the River Balvag, lies Beinn an t-Sidhein, 'the hill of the fairies'. Perhaps it is an indication of the unfortunate trend in anglicizing the old Gaelic names that the Forestry Commission has insisted on signposting the hill as Ben Shian and that a hotel in Strathyre is called the Ben Sheann Hotel. This is an unfortunate trend and, in the long run, doesn't help visitors understand the meaning of the Gaelic. The word 'sith', meaning 'fairy', is a word that walkers come across quite often in Scotland. The derivative 'shian' or 'sheann' tends to confuse and reduces the colourful, and often beautiful, Gaelic names to nondescript abbreviations.

My route lay across the ridge of this hill, over to the farm at Ballimore, and then to Balquhidder, the final resting-place of Rob Roy. A good footpath climbs up through the forest plantation on the eastern slopes of Beinn an t-Sidhein – steep in places, but it gains height fast. It was another good day of brilliant sunshine, and the dew had left cobwebs of silver patterns on the trees and heather. The track peters out shortly after leaving the forest, high on the ridge, but a series of marker posts points the way down into Glen Buckie. To the north-west the Braes o' Balquhidder, celebrated in Robert Tannahill's song of the same name, dominated the view, pockmarked with the remnants of winter snow.

The second day of the route is an easy one after the long 18 miles (29 km) of the first day. The walk over Beinn an t-Sidhein completes the climbing for the day; the rest of the day is a happy stravaig down to Balquhidder, then a lochside stroll up the glen beyond Inverlochlarig, a day of gentler scenery and history tinged with sadness as we pass Rob Roy's last home at Inverlochlarig.

From the farm at Ballimore in Glen Buckie, a two-mile (three-km) stretch of road takes you downhill to the small village of Balquhidder, where Rob Roy is buried.

The kirk of Balquhidder is an extremely picturesque one. Standing on a grassy knoll above the Kirkton, it offers a superb panorama of the Balquhidder glen. There are actually two churchyards; the original kirk, which dates from 1631, is now a ruin, and the new church stands behind it. The grave of the Macgregor chief is in fact unknown, but three monuments allegedly cover the final resting-places of Rob, his wife Mary (called Helen by Scott) and two of their sons, Coll and Robin. The stones are typical late Scottish medieval – there is no doubt about that – and the third stone certainly covers a Macgregor, as it displays the clan crest of a sword, a crown and a pine tree which has been torn up by its roots, the uprooted pine symbolizing the tragic misfortunes of the proscribed clan.

Returning to the southern shore of Loch Voil, back across the triple-arched Balvag Bridge, I stopped for a moment to take in the view down the loch, one of the finest in the southern Highlands. Loch Voil has tiny wooded islands, promontories winding into the water, and on either bank are steep-sided hills stretching back, fold upon fold, into the jumble of high mountains that fade into the far west.

Just as the farm buildings of Muirlaggan came into view, a track, not marked on my map, broke off uphill. A signpost said 'Hikers This Way'. After climbing for a couple of hundred feet, the track then ran parallel to the Muirlaggan one on the shoreline and continued for another mile and a half. The track was obviously bulldozed to service what appears to be a holiday cottage, a timber building, which, in the afternoon sun, looked alpine in appearance. The track ended here, and I had to decide whether to maintain height and try to find a way through the forestry plantation or drop down and chance my luck with the shoreline. I dropped down to the loch – down steepish heathery slopes, and immediately came upon a faint track running between the trees and the shingly shore. Although wet and boggy in places, it was far preferable to negotiating the deep furrows and prickly pines of the forest plantation higher up the hill.

Loch Voil and Loch Doine are virtually one loch. Only a narrow spit of land and a short stretch of slow-moving river separates the two. In his book *The Scottish Lochs* Tom Weir explains that the separation of the two lochs was due to a build-up of alluvium from the Monachyle Burn in the north and the Monachyle Tuarach in the south working towards each other.

The farmhouse at Monachyle Tuarach was Rob Roy's first steading, a gift from his father in 1692. Because of the farm's unsuitability for arable farming, Rob decided to concentrate on sheep, soon becoming a well-known figure at the markets and trysts throughout Scotland. It was to here that Rob brought his young wife, Mary Macgregor of Comar, a distant cousin.

The track continued alongside Loch Doine, and across the loch the long craggy slopes of Stob Binnein and Beinn Tulaichean rose high, two popular Munros. At the head of the loch stands the farm of Inverlochlarig, built on the site of the house in which Rob Roy died on 27 December 1734. It was a peaceful death, so uncharacteristic after a life of adventure and turmoil. As he lay on his deathbed, he was informed that a MacLaren had come to pay his respects. Not wanting to be seen by an erstwhile enemy in his bedclothes, Rob commanded his family to dress him in his plaid and to gather his weapons around him. He thus greeted his visitor. When the MacLaren left, Rob lifted himself up on his elbows and asked his piper to play the lament 'Cha till mi Tuiidh' – 'I Shall Return No More'. Before the piper had finished, Rob had passed away. His body was carried in great ceremony and mourning to Balquhidder, where he was buried.

Leaving Inverlochlarig, I began the last stretch of the pilgrimage of the Fiery Cross; back through the hills to Loch Katrine-side. It was now late afternoon, so I decided to head through the high pass of the Glen of Weeping, which skirts the western slopes of Stob a' Choin. The drooping sun was casting long shadows on the surrounding hills and a curlew called in the distance. I almost expected to hear a lonely pibroch drift in

the air from the glen, but only the sound of the curlew broke the stillness, a sound comparable in sadness and expression. I camped on the 1000-foot (305-m) contour close to a small lochan and lay in the tent doorway to watch the sky turn orange, crimson and then violet before the glimmer of the first star heralded darkness.

The Glen of Weeping to Trossachs Pier

•

I woke early to a thin drizzle. Two stags were grazing contentedly about a hundred yards away, oblivious to my presence. They didn't look my way once, until my petrol stove roared into life and sent them bounding up the opposite slope. After breakfast the weather began to clear, and a watery sun tried to ooze from a leaden sky. I made my way over boggy ground by the Allt a' Choin, a meandering hill stream that flows southwards into Loch Katrine, possibly the most beautiful of the Trossachs lochs. As usual, Sir Walter Scott summed it up succinctly in only four lines:

> *High in the south huge Ben Venue,*
> *Down on the lake in masses threw,*
> *Crags, knolls, and mounds, confusedly hurled,*
> *the fragments of an earlier world.*

The final stretch of the route is about six to seven miles (nine and a half to eleven km) along a tarmac private road, and despite the false tidiness of this road-bound northern shore, the view across the loch to Ellen's Isle and Ben Venue is still wild and wondrous. Below Ben Venue an ancient pass slices through the hillside – the Bealach nam Bo, where the Gregorach drove their stolen cattle en route to Glengyle at the head of Loch Katrine. Below the bealach lies the Coire nan Uruisgean, 'corrie of the urisks', or 'goblins', reputedly the meeting place for all the goblins in Scotland, who gathered here to plan and plot amid the deep heather and boulder-scarred hollows. These urisks, explains Dr Graham in his *Scenery of the Southern Confines of Perthshire*, published in 1806, 'were a sort of lubbery supernatural, who could be gained over by kind attention to perform the drudgery of a farm. They were supposed to be spread throughout the Highlands each in his own wild recess, but the solemn meetings of the order were regularly held in this cave of Benvenew.'

Left: Loch Katrine from the lower slopes of Ben Venue

•

It was early afternoon as I approached the pier and the end of my walk. There were dozens of people about, parking their cars in the car park at the pier and walking a few dozen yards down the lochside before scampering back again, scratching at the edges of what the Trossachs has to offer. I reached my car, put my pack in the boot, feeling richer for the experience of following in the footsteps of history. More important, I felt I had experienced something of the rich tapestry of Scottish history that had so inspired and motivated that wonderful writer Sir Walter Scott.

CHAPTER FOUR

GLEN NEVIS

SOLITUDE ON THE HIGH TOPS

•

Cameron McNeish

A three-day walk around the skyline of Glen Nevis, climbing over Ben Nevis, the Aonachs, the Grey Corries and the Mamores

---

MAP: *OS 1:50 000 Sheet 41*
START: *Achintee Farm, Glen Nevis. Grid ref:125730*
FINISH: *Youth Hostel, Glen Nevis. Grid ref: 127717*
LENGTH: *Approximately 40 miles (64 km)*
APPROXIMATE TIME: *3 days*
TERRAIN: *Difficult mountain-walking over a remote and unrelenting landscape*
ACCOMMODATION: *Hotels, guest-houses and b&bs in Fort William. Youth hostel in Glen Nevis. Commercial campsite in Glen Nevis. Ben Nevis bunkhouse at Achintee Farm*

Like many folk, I have a love–hate relationship with Ben Nevis. To stand on its summit, at 4408 feet (1343 m) above the tidal waters that lap the urban shores of Fort William, the high point of a largish plateau of scree and stones, is as close as most of us are likely to get to heaven, at least in the UK. But the summit of Ben Nevis is far from divine. Indeed, these grim acres have been described as the highest midden in Britain.

An orange-coloured Nissen hut dominates the top, no doubt serving its purpose as an emergency shelter in an eyeball-searing sort of way. All around it stones are piled into indiscriminate cairns, some of them bearing inconsequential memorial plaques, while others are merely there for the same reasons as a dog pees up against a tree – to leave a sign of its passing.

The ruins of another building, the old Weather Observatory, bear testament to the bold characters who worked here at the end of the nineteenth century, collecting and collating meteorological data, but like the tacky memorial cairns the remains offer a sad monument – only ruined walls remain, their dereliction a sure sign that buildings

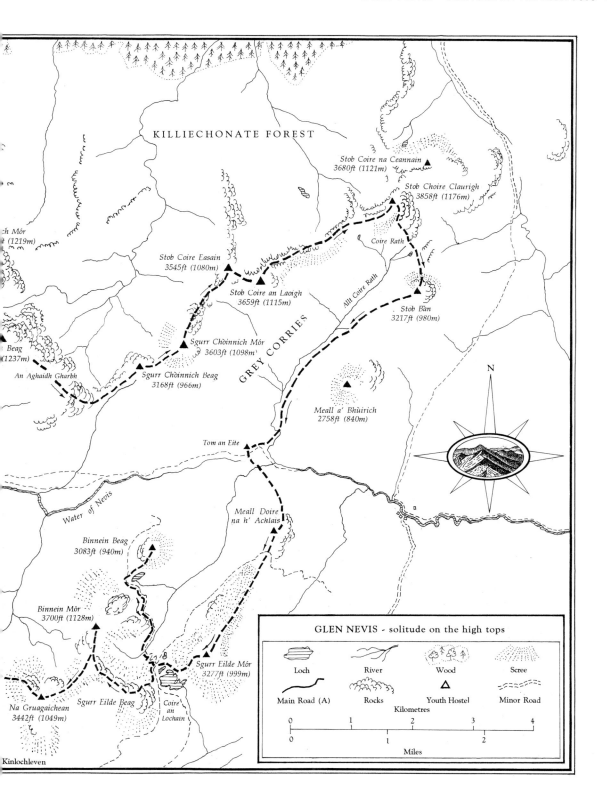

KILLIECHONATE FOREST

Stob Coire na Ceannain
3680ft (1121m)

Stob Choire Claurigh
3858ft (1176m)

Coire Rath

ch Mór
(1219m)

Stob Coire Easain
3545ft (1080m)

Stob Coire an Laoigh
3659ft (1115m)

Stob Bàn
3217ft (980m)

Beag
(1237m)

An Aghaidh Gharbh

Sgurr Chòinnich Mór
3603ft (1098m)

Sgurr Chòinnich Beag
3168ft (966m)

GREY CORRIES

Meall a' Bhùirich
2758ft (840m)

N

Tom an Eite

Water of Nevis

Meall Doire
na h' Achlais

Binnein Beag
3083ft (940m)

Binnein Mór
3700ft (1128m)

Sgurr Eilde Mór
3277ft (999m)

Na Gruagaichean
3442ft (1049m)

Sgurr Eilde Beag

Coire
an
Lochain

Kinlochleven

GLEN NEVIS - solitude on the high tops

Loch	River	Wood	Scree
Main Road (A)	Rocks	Youth Hostel	Minor Road

Kilometres

0   1   2   3   4

0   1   2

Miles

won't, can't, survive in the face of such climatic hostility. Records from the old station suggest the name Ben Nevis could translate as 'venomous mountain'; it has a mean annual rainfall of 157 inches (399 cm), with a maximum of 240 inches (610 cm), a mean monthly temperature half a degree below freezing; snow can fall on any day of the year, and the permanent winter fall often begins in October. The summit has an average of 261 gales each year, many of them reaching hurricane force, often with gusts of 150mph (240kph) in winter. 'Venomous mountain' seems appropriate…

This loose interpretation of the name matched my humour. Too many demands on my time by other people had left me ragged and curmudgeonly, and I had become aware of the need to isolate myself for a time. It was a familiar exigency – its echoes had been sounding loudly – and the best thing I could do was take myself off for a few days and immerse myself in the mountain's boundaries. I wanted to regulate my privacy. I needed space where my mind could enjoy the luxury of thinking through a single chain of thoughts to a logical conclusion without interruption. Most of all I wanted to escape from the schedules and timetables invariably imposed on me by other people, and long experience had taught me that a very desirable aspect of retreating to what we call wilderness is that doing so allowed me to control what I want to pay attention to. What I needed was a place where I could choose what to do and what not to do, even if that were something as mundane as lying on a sunlit hillside contemplating my navel. The choices and the actions and the responsibilities were mine and mine alone – there is a novelty in that sort of simplicity which never fails to appeal, time and time again.

Achintee to the Grey Corries
•

The track from Achintee in Glen Nevis to the summit of Ben Nevis, unless it is your first time and you desperately want to reach the summit of Britain's highest mountain, falls into the dull category. The western and southern aspects of Ben Nevis reflect this dullness: rounded, hunched, rising above a coterie of more shapely neighbours, and the old Pony Track, originally built to service the meteorological station that once graced the summit, takes the line of least resistance. Nowadays this long route to the summit is called the Tourist Track, and it robs walkers of the sight of Ben Nevis's redeeming feature, the long line of buttresses, ridges, crags and faces held in the clench of its north-east-facing corries, the 2000-foot-high (610-m-high) barricade of cliffs which offers the best snow- and ice-climbing in the country. To catch a glimpse of the Ben's true character you have to combine its ascent with that of Carn Mór Dearg, which lies to the north. That was my next destination.

The Achintee track runs for about five miles (eight km) to the summit of the Ben, a long relentless pull from just above sea-level to 4408 feet (1343 m), the highest point of land in Britain. The track first of all winds around the shoulder of Meall an t-Suidhe, the Ben's westerly neighbour, to the Half-Way Lochan and then, by a series of zigzags and a hideous line of waymarking cairns, it makes its way up the steep western shoulder of stony screes to the summit plateau. Everything about this route, and its summit destination, cries out against the reasons most of us climb mountains, but at least Ben Nevis has been spared the ignominy of having a train running up its flanks. So far…

Solitude is a rare privilege on top of Ben Nevis in summer, and already people were congregating around the summit cairn and Observatory ruins. On my ascent I had probably passed, and been passed by, several hundred folk, and I realized that if I wanted quiet isolation then the best thing I could do was to keep walking. I didn't linger. Despite anything else the weather was far too chilly for me to hang around, even in late May, and the grey cloud covering everything was damp. I scurried off towards the scree slopes that lead in a south-easterly direction towards the Carn Mór Dearg arête and better backpacking hills. Care was required in the mist to find the correct route as a course held for too long to the east can lead into difficulties at the top of the often-frozen slopes that drop off into upper Coire Leis.

Almost immediately I felt better. Ten minutes of descent on rough, loose scree brought me below cloud-level and there in front of me lay my route for the next couple of days – a traverse of the Aonachs, the Grey Corries, across the watershed of Tom an Eite and back along the huge switchbacked ridges of the Mamores. The planned route was about 40 miles (64 km), with a good 20 000 feet (6095 m) of climbing, and I was going to tackle it the easy way. The late Philip Tranter, son of the Scottish novelist and historian Nigel Tranter, was the first person to waltz around this self-same route inside 24 hours, an astonishing time even for someone in his twenties – although his feat paled to some insignificance when it was repeated a few years later by a lady in her mid-fifties.

A small burrow among the rocks looked like a good spot for lunch and an opportunity for the thought processes to begin. All the way up the Ben my brain had been hammering out a whole sequence of thoughts and sensations, a mêlée of concepts and notions that had failed to sort themselves into any logical sequence or satisfactory conclusions. But this is always the way of it at the start of a long walk, and one of the great delights of escaping to green places is that while we walk, or sit quietly in the sun, we have time actually to follow our thoughts. Phones don't ring, visitors don't intrude. Even if only for a few hours, we can count on that time as our own, and what is important is not really what we think but the fact that we are free to think, without interruption.

I moved off after lunch and almost immediately the Carn Mór Dearg arête demanded my full attention. This high arête leads you along a rocky tightrope to the red-hued summit slopes of Carn Mór Dearg, a graceful, sensual curve of rock which forms the south-west wall of Coire Leis. At close quarters the ridge is broader than it first appears

ABOVE: BEN NEVIS FROM THE AIR

RIGHT: THE FINE SWEEP OF THE CARN MÓR DEARG ARÊTE

•

and a footpath has been worn along its eastern edge. The arête itself is made up of a series of piled blocks which makes a more exciting highway than the footpath. Narrow and marginally exposed, there are few difficulties, and the exhilaration of its traverse never fails to obliterate the shadowy thoughts cast by Ben Nevis's growing urbanization.

As I crossed this slender tendon between the Ben and the rest of my route, something astonishing but not wholly unexpected occurred. It was a moment I was waiting for, a moment I always expect at some point on a trip like this – the mental breakthrough between one world and the next; between the everyday, routine world of timetables, deadlines, responsibilities and everything else that makes up my world and the world I was seeking for a few days, the natural world of hills and mountains, grass and heather, rock and crashing mountain streams. Sometimes it's an encounter with wildlife that opens the door; at other times the breakthrough comes at a time of sustained effort. And yet again, it often happens as I move from one type of landscape to another, like walking through a mist from one time-zone into another. The end result is always the same, a feeling – no, an awareness – that once again I've become part of what I'm moving through, part again of that intricate web of a huge ecosystem of which we understand so little. These days will refresh me and quicken my spirit in preparation for my return.

A long stony slope links the end of the arête with Carn Mór Dearg's summit, and I took the opportunity to dawdle and once again appreciate this other aspect of Ben Nevis's schizophrenic character. Across the gulf of the corrie of the Allt a' Muilinn, two miles (three km) of cliffs, buttresses, ridges and crags arrayed themselves in naked display. As though a scalpel had sliced through the mountain, Ben Nevis was baring its innards, revealing its heart. Outpourings of scree and boulders gave way to gullies and snow chutes, the remnants of the winter revealing the serried nature of the cliffs, riven and scarred by steep, tortuous lines that attracted the best mountaineers of the world. This is surely the beating heart of Ben Nevis, the playground of climbers, scramblers and mountaineers and all who appreciate such form and splendour.

I lingered by Carn Mór Dearg's summit, wrapped up in my new-found release. The question I had asked earlier still flirted with me. What is it about isolation that appears so attractive when life becomes too busy? Is it simply escapism? I suppose it is, but there's also a form of self-regulation that we can create when we feel we're on the edge of being engulfed by circumstances.

Getting away from it all is simply that – an escape from a place where there is the threat of control to a place where you can be in charge of your own decisions and experiences. I guess you could call it freedom – one of the most sought-after rights of any human being on earth.

It was only two o'clock and I looked forward to ambling slowly over Aonach Mór and Aonach Beag, the two bulky hills that rise due east of Carn Mór Dearg. These hills are something of a Gaelic anomaly: Aonach Mór, 'the big ridge', is 3999 feet (1219 m) above sea-level, while Aonach Beag, 'the small ridge', is 4060 feet (1237 m). Their heights prove only that the folk who named these hills did so from the perspective of their bulk and mass rather than their height above sea-level. In this respect, Aonach Mór certainly is larger. The height and numbers game is a fairly recent phenomenon, and although most folk would agree that mountain-bagging is intrinsically daft it is addictive in its own way.

A long, steep and stony ridge drops off eastwards towards the high bealach below Aonach Mór, the high point of an ancient through route from Steall to Torlundy on General Wade's military road, built in the eighteenth century to subdue the troublesome Highland clans. The bealach is a moody and atmospheric spot, lochan-splattered and usually boggy, where the craggy western slopes of Aonach Mór force you southeastwards on a steep traverse to gain the rough slopes that give access to a higher and less dour bealach, the shallow col between the two Aonachs. The summit of Aonach Mór demanded an out-and-back from the col. The mountain itself has fallen prey to the ski business, and while many walkers now ascend it from the north by way of the relatively new gondola system, I was happy to avoid the ski detritus.

The summit ridge of Aonach Mór is gravelly, with long steep drops on either side. I was back in the cloud again, the wraith-like fingers of damp hurrying me along, no lingering, just a visit to the summit cairn and a backtrack to the bealach. I was now anxious to get over Aonach Beag, a tricky hill in the mist, as quickly as possible. A steeper, stony climb led to the small cairn that marks the top of Aonach Beag and I reached it in good time. I had been on this hill several times before, but usually in good weather, and now that I was here in thick cloud the words of mountaineer Hamish Brown kept floating through my mind. In his book *Hamish's Mountain Walk*, he advised: 'This is not a good area to wander about in if there is thick cloud, not unless you have a parachute.' Steep cliffs fall sharply away to the north-east into the An Aghaidh Gharbh, and the rounded dome of the summit is pretty featureless.

My route was now an easterly one, a direction that was made awkward by a series of steep cliffs falling away steeply into a large corrie. I knew that a rough route existed down through the cliffs, but the mist prevented me from relating to familiar features. Unwilling to take unnecessary risks, I made my way alongside the clifftops to a subsidiary top at the eastern end of the ridge and managed to make my way carefully and slowly down through the crags and outcrops to a high grassy bealach below Sgurr Chòinnich Beag. I could now relax.

It was almost six o'clock. I decided to stop on the flattish bealach for the night. The next stretch of the walk was a five-mile (eight-km) ridge walk along the crests of the Grey Corries and I didn't really see much point in bashing along them in cloud. Water ran from a spring not far below me, I was below the cloud-line, a square of green turf presented a welcoming face and I knew this was my room for the night.

Looking towards the Mamores and
Glen Coe hills from the Grey Corries

As usual, it was good to stop. The joys of backpacking can be experienced in simple things – the relative weightlessness when you ease the pack from your shoulders; the removal of a sweat-soaked and inevitably smelly shirt and replacing it with a clean, dry one; and best of all the luxurious sensation of peeling off socks from feet that are hot and sore. I could now lie back and gaze out of my tent door at mountains that seemed to flow on to eternity. Always, always preferable to the confining walls of a bothy or hostel. All the mountains I could see were decapitated by the low cloud-level: Binnein Beag and Mór, the start of the long Mamores chain, my hills for the day after tomorrow, and beyond the long wall of the Aonach Eagach which forms the northern jaws of distant Glen Coe. To the north stretched the great wilderness of mountains beyond the Great Glen, the Loch Arkaig hills, the Loch Quoich set, Affric, Kintail and Torridon, a litany of names and memories.

A soft breeze rustled the fabric of the tent, and once I had eaten and washed up I lay outside for a while. A goodly snort of whisky kept me company, and it didn't take long for the alcohol to agitate the simmering emotions that are always stirred by nights like this. The peace, the beauty, the feeling of belonging and an almost overwhelming sensation of blessing never fail to humble me on these occasions. And once again I was glad to be on my own. I'm not ashamed to admit it but there are times when I cry because of the stark, simple beauty of my surroundings, and at times like this I want to distance myself from others. Inevitably, this sort of feeling largely depends on your personality. Extroverts won't care if others see them crying or rejoicing in extravagant fashion, but others may be more self-conscious about such a show and seek an out-of-the-way retreat.

When my father died suddenly I, the eldest son, had a number of responsibilites to attend to. I had to show a brave face, even though inside I was in turmoil. It wasn't until after the funeral, alone with my wife, that I broke down and cried. Grief poured from me like a torrent, and with the defensive wall broken the mourning process could begin. But I needed that comparative solitude, away from friends and family. Alone, with only my wife, that relative isolation became the vehicle for the personal, cathartic, emotional release that was so necessary at that time, an isolation that allowed me space in which to fully consider the sudden loss of my father and my emotional response, just as the isolation of a high-level mountain camp allowed me full rein to the emotional responses that are stirred by natural beauty, peace and silence.

The Grey Corries to Sgurr Eilde Mór
•

I was away by eight o'clock after a quick breakfast of cereal and coffee. The cloud had crept down during the night and enveloped my tent in a damp, grey shroud, but as I lay in my sleeping-bag in that half-conscious state between sleep and wakefulness, dribbling coffee down my beard like an idiot, I was aware of an unearthly, luminous light in the tent. I poked my head outside to see the cloud miraculously lift before my eyes, like a curtain going up on a wonderful stage of rock and grass, peak and sky. The still-veiled sun was already warming the air. No time to linger in bed, there was now a prospect of early-morning views, usually the finest of all.

The Grey Corries take their name from their caps of silver quartzite, and they are marvellous hills to walk. Only the peaks of the north-facing corries are silver in appearance, and they are connected by a long and switchbacked ridge that meanders its way over three Munros: Sgurr Chòinnich Mór (3603 feet/1098 m), Stob Coire an Laoigh (3659ft/1115 m), unnamed on the OS 1:50 000 sheet, and Stob Choire Claurigh (3858 feet/1176 m). An afterthought to the main Grey Corries ridge, Stob Bàn, at 3217 feet (980 m), is also a Munro. The first top, Sgurr Chòinnich Beag, 'the small mossy peak', gave a good warm-up for the day over short, brownish turf, and the bigger mossy peak, Sgurr Chòinnich Mór, heralded the start of the ridge proper.

As a ridge walk the traverse of the Grey Corries is not unduly difficult, with few obstacles to cause concern to the backpacker. But the views of the ridge itself, and of its near and far neighbours, the dazzling effects of the sun squinting off the snow-white crests, the exquisite formation of the graceful curves of the corrie rims, and the breath-taking impressions of the great height above Glen Nevis in the south and Glen Spean in the north make it a wonderful expedition.

A slight breeze was cool enough to be comfortable, and I was oblivious to the weight of my pack as I strode from top to top. Stob Coire Easain came and went, and still the ridge billowed on in undulating waves. A turn to the south-east gave me the unnamed Munro which is Stob Coire an Laoigh, 'the hill of the corrie of the calves', and going over the subsidiary tops towards Stob Choire Claurigh I met my first fellow walkers of the day. I was a little startled to see them: although it was less than 24 hours since I had seen other people, I was already deep in the solitude mind-set. I nodded, grunted a brief little homily about the weather and scampered on.

A little further on I stopped for a break. Below me, tiny glaciated lochans sparkled like diamonds in the sun, a herd of deer moved across the slopes like a cloud shadow, and from somewhere much closer a lark twittered enthusiastically. Across Coire Rath, the little dumpy peak of Stob Bàn, an addendum to the main Grey Corries ridge, looked comfortingly small. I had made good time on the ridges, and there and then decided that after reaching Stob Choire Claurigh I would traverse Stob Bàn and wander up the slopes of Sgurr Eilde Mór which lay across the glen to the south. Just as Stob Bàn is an afterthought to the Grey Corries ridge, so Sgurr Eilde Mór is tacked onto the Mamores. I knew of a delectable camping spot beside a high-level lochan on the southern flank of the hill which would give me a bracing start to the Binneins, Mór and Beag, the beginning of the Mamore ridge proper, the next morning. That would

Above: Looking towards Sgurr a' Mhàim
from Na Gruagaichean

Right: Loch Eilde Mór, cosily snuggled between high hills

•

give me 12 miles (19 km) and some 4500 feet (1372 m) of climbing for the day, and that didn't sound too bad at all.

Stob Choire Claurigh is the highest of the Grey Corries, and from its summit I gazed back along the silver switchbacks to the great gully-seamed cliffs of the Aonachs and beyond them, in all its elevated glory, the great hunchback of Ben Nevis, its rounded top now clear of cloud and its black cliffs as awesome as ever. The route lay steeply downhill now, and it felt odd to be climbing down to collect the Munro of Stob Bàn, a curious sensation but a nice one at this stage in the day. Scree rolled below my feet as I trundled down, past the little lochan on the bealach, over a rocky bump and onto the very loose scree-covered slopes of Stob Bàn.

The obvious route of descent looked as if it went south, over the intervening hump of Meall a' Bhùirich, but feeling in a perverse frame of mind I instead followed the broad grassy slopes of Stob Bàn south-westwards into Coire Rath to where its stream, the Allt Coire Rath, ran its tumultuous course down to the humpy, bumpy moraines of Tom an Eite. I suppose you could describe Tom an Eite as a shallow col, but it's so shallow that it appears to hold the waters from a thousand streams in its cusp. In all my experiences of walking and climbing in the Scottish Highlands, this is the wettest place I know. I wanted to stop for a while and have a brew, but I couldn't find a dry place to sit! The boggy morass quivered as I tiptoed tentatively from tussock to tussock and almost inevitably it wasn't long before I went in up to the knees. After that I simply spludged on through the bogs in a perversely triumphant attitude. It would soon be time to camp for the night, and I had dry socks in my pack.

To the south, the long whaleback ridge of Sgurr Eilde Mór rises from its prominent subsidiary Meall Doire na h'Achlais in a very gentle curve to its broad top at 3279 feet (999 m). Its easy slopes and long broad ridge present few difficulties, although the descent from the summit into Coire an Lochain, where I intended to camp, is fairly steep. Some measure of care would be required.

The lochan, or more correctly the large lochan and its two or three smaller dependants, snuggle cosily in the high, flat bealach between the steep, crumbly southern slopes of Sgurr Eilde Mór and the even steeper black crags of Sgurr Eilde Beag, which is actually more of a subsidiary top of Binnein Mór than a top in its own right. Twenty-odd deer bounded off towards Binnein Beag as I disturbed their early-evening reverie and gulls screeched noisily from the still surface of the lochans, pointing out their concern at my noisy intrusion. Just as I had pitched the tent and was organizing the stove for a brew, a long and mournful wail sounded from the opposite side of the loch, a long, rising cry that brought a shiver to my spine – the sombre cry of a diver, probably a red-throated diver. It was an eerie sound in the stillness of the evening, a true cry of the wilderness spirit. The call of a brother being. I wasn't really alone.

I had read a book recently called *Biophilia*, which looked in some detail at the bond we humans have with other species. The author, a Harvard sociobiologist by the name of Edward O. Wilson, made a statement which sounded to me like profound wisdom: 'Wilderness settles peace on the soul because it needs no help. It is beyond human contrivance.' Beyond human contrivance. That simple statement struck a chord with me. It spoke to me of eternal values, things that have always been, as ancient as the duration of days. The call of the red-throated diver or the screech of the gulls or the movement of red deer hinds across the hillside are all completely and utterly unplanned – not one of these things has been engineered, or created, or rehearsed by man, and that, I think, is the nub of the matter. There is a tangible comfort in that. The human spirit needs places where nature has not been rearranged by man. Gardens and parks are fine in themselves, but as more and more people are testifying we need more than that – we need wild places, and the reason our spirit demands them is because all the chaos and trauma of modern life can make sense only when you are willing to stand back and view them from a different angle, from the mountains, the sea, the forests and the wide-open skies, from the natural world itself.

Tonight, the natural world cried out in all its quiet beauty, and I went off to bed with the sound of it ringing in my ears.

Sgurr Eilde Mór to Glen Nevis

The morning broke breezy but thankfully clear. I quickly found the old stalkers' path that runs around the western slopes of the bealach and leads to the small lochan which nestles below the symmetrical cone shape of Binnein Beag. I dumped my pack beside the lochan and climbed the steep, shingly quartzite to the summit cairn. Like Stob Bàn, Binnein Beag (3083 feet/940 m) is an addendum to the main Mamore ridge and almost looks too small to be a Munro, but it does offer very fine views of its bigger neighbours. There are nine Munros on the Mamores ridge, a great incentive to Munro-baggers to hike the whole of the ridge in one go, but few do. The narrow crests demand careful attention and concentration, and one or two short sections of ridge require the use of hands, but despite the odd bit of scrambling these are undoubtedly walkers' hills, one of the finest ridge walks in the country.

I descended to the lochan again and collected my pack. A steep and rocky north ridge leads to the narrow summit ridge of Binnein Mór, at 3700 feet (1128 m) the highest of the Mamores and a superb vantage point. On a good day you can see from Cruachan in the south-west to Torridon in the north. The actual summit is a little way out on a limb from the main ridge, and I enjoyed the breezy half-mile or so southwards to gain the main Mamore ridge. The ridge, which had broadened out on Binnein Mór's southern summit, soon narrowed again on the approach to the twin-topped

Na Gruagaichean, 'the maiden', at 3442 feet (1049 m), its twin paps a quarter of a mile or so apart. The southern top is the higher, with a drop of about 200 feet (60 m) before you begin climbing the narrow ridge to the second top. Na Gruagaichean is perched high above the village of Kinlochleven in the south and allows good views over the Devil's Staircase to Rannoch Moor and the steep-sided flanks of the Buachaille Etive Mór, guardian of both Glen Etive and Glen Coe.

The next top on the ridge to the north-west was Stob Coire a' Chairn (unnamed on the 1:50 000 map). The main ridge swings south-west from Stob Coire a' Chairn towards Am Bodach, 'the old man', but two outliers to the north, An Garbhanach and An Gearanach, the rough and the short ridge, provide an exhilarating packless scramble. The ridge between the two is tightrope stuff, a heady ridge with steep, grassy slopes falling away on either side.

The next Munro on the ridge, Am Bodach (3383 feet/1031 m), sits proudly at the head of Coire a'Mhàil. A stalkers' track skirts across the lower slopes of the hill to reach the main ridge of Sgurr an Iubhair further on, but I climbed on through the rough broken crags and through a succession of loose scree gullies to gain the summit. It was worth it to get good views across to Ben Nevis and the graceful curving sweep of the Carn Mór Dearg arête. The ridge then runs easily down to a 2800-foot (853-m) saddle, giving views across to Stob Bàn and Mullach nan Coirean in the distance. To the south, the blue waters of Loch Leven glinted in the sun, and the long barrier of the Aonach Eagach ridge, culminating in the rounded wart of the Pap of Glencoe, was backed by the peaks of the Bidean nam Bian massif. The ridge began rising again over white screes to Sgurr an Iubhair, 'the peak of the yew', again not named on the map. This peak, like Stob Coire a' Chairn, has a northern outlier of Munro status, Sgurr a' Mhàim, the hill that totally dominates Glen Nevis when seen from the lower reaches of the glen. Like its eastern neighbours Gearanach and Garbhanach, it lies at the end of a very narrow ridge, alarmingly named the Devil's Ridge. In winter, under conditions of snow and ice, it can be a formidable proposition, but in summer it is no worse than the Gearanach ridge. It's not to be missed, especially if you can leave your pack by the cairn on Sgurr an Iubhair and cross the ridge unladen. Two-thirds of the way across, a series of rocks forms the crest of the ridges with a safe path running around them on the eastern side. Without the weight of a pack fighting me, I scrambled my way over the tops of the rocks, elementary rock-scrambling, and reached the slopes to Sgurr a' Mhàim twittering in delight. It was so good I went back the same way!

I stopped by my pack and took a little break, still exhilarated by my scrambles. Although physically I felt a little tired, I was aware of the mental release that these days had given me. I could now think clearly, I felt more focused and suddenly life felt optimistic again. I suppose another aspect of physical removal from society into nature is the mental view. Anne LaBastille is an American writer who has looked at this whole question in some detail. She's written that the greatest value wilderness has to

THE MAMORE RIDGE, THE NARROW CRESTS CALLING FOR CARE AND CONCENTRATION

•

humankind is the healing of psychological wounds, and mountains, lakes and forests could well become our psychiatrists. Can you imagine it? Stress therapy will be solitude and silence scheduled at regular intervals. The late Edward Abbey, author, erstwhile park ranger and champion of the American south-west, once wrote: 'We need wilderness whether or not we ever set foot in it. We need the possibility of escape as surely as we need hope; without it the life of the cities would drive all men into crime, drugs or psychoanalysis. The natural environment has the power to set one's mind at peace and give hope to a sometimes dreary world.'

Regulating one's need for isolation, finding appropriate locations for isolation and understanding one's own desires for isolation can help individuals define their need for privacy. The whole subject of isolation is much more exhaustive than I've suggested in the course of this route, but getting away from it all is becoming more and more important to many of us, and, I suspect, should be taken much more seriously.

I was beginning to feel tired. All the Mamore Munros in a day is a hefty hike, and I still had two to go. Stob Bàn, a beautiful hill, is a shapely peak of predominantly ash-grey quartz, hence its name, the White Hill. I struggled up its rocky slopes slowly and deliberately, fully aware that the last Munro of the day, Mullach nan Coirean, was still a long way off. At the summit I took a five-minute break and gazed back along the ridge. Binnein Mór stood out impressively above the others; it seemed a long way back, but I was homeward bound now, heading off northwards, then due west along the Stob Bàn ridge until I came across the lip of the huge eastern corrie of the last Munro. I followed the cliff edge around past the south-east top and then a descent, then a reascent to the broad, flat summit ridge. No sharp conical peak here, but a flat plateau-like summit, difficult to navigate in mist. The wind was really picking up now, and every step was becoming a battle on the exposed summit ridge. Three thousand feet (914 m) below lay Glen Nevis and home, and rather than struggle down the steep slopes directly below me, I followed the well-defined north ridge towards the minor top of Sgorr Chalum. The easy and gently sloping ridge was a surprise, a delight to wander down. A forest firebreak led through the conifer plantation, and very quickly I found myself back on the Glen Nevis road, a mile or so south of the youth hostel where I had left my car. People milled around, cars drove past in a steady line, but I was ready for them all now, ready to take my place in society again, at least for a while.

CHAPTER FIVE

THE CAIRNGORMS

LINKING THE TWO LAIRIGS

•

Cameron McNeish

*A three-day walk around the Cairngorms, linking the Lairig Ghru and the
lesser-known Lairig an Laoigh*

MAP: *OS 1:50 000 Sheet 36*
START: *B970 at Coylumbridge, near Aviemore. Grid Ref: 915107*
FINISH: *Glenmore Lodge. Grid Ref: 987096*
LENGTH: *About 40 miles (64 km)*
APPROXIMATE TIME: *3 days*
TERRAIN: *Mostly on paths and tracks but the route visits some isolated and remote areas. The Cairngorms are
regarded as having an Arctic climate, so snow can fall at any time of the year. Not a route for the inexperienced or
for those who can't navigate*
ACCOMMODATION: *Hotels, guest-houses and b&bs in Aviemore. There is also a youth hostel. Glenmore Lodge,
at the end of the route, has a public bar*

Our mountains, generally speaking, are shrinking. Through the aeons of time they are gradually being ground down by the scouring action of water, frost and wind. It's a long, slow process of gradual destruction, but the Cairngorms are different. These are mountains of circum-denudation – that is, while they have been carved out of their original plateau blocks by erosion, now the course of fast-flowing waters in the valleys and glens will largely dictate their future shaping and remoulding. The future of the Cairngorms is in the hands of the bubbling burns, the chattering streams and the wide, stately rivers.

These burns, streams and rivers of the Cairngorms make up a radial drainage system. From a solid granite centre, the waters flow outwards in every direction, but because the central Cairngorm massif has a slight south-eastern tilt, that tends to be the predominant direction of the major watercourses: the River Dee, which in its infant

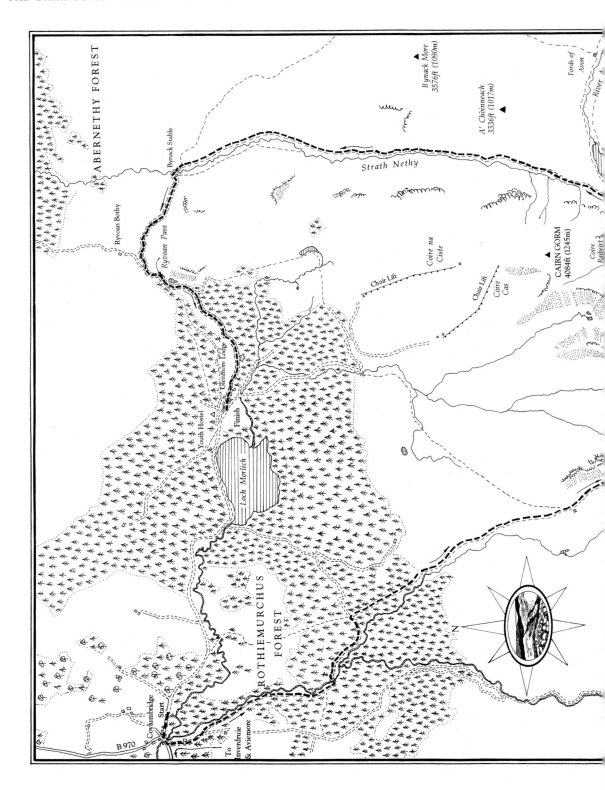

ABERNETHY FOREST

Bynack More
3576ft (1090m)

A' Chòinneach
3336ft (1017m)

Fords of
Avon

River

Bynack Stable

Strath Nethy

Ryvoan Bothy

Ryvoan Pass

Coire na
Ciste

Chair Lift

CAIRN GORM
4084ft (1245m)

Coire
Raibert

Chair Lift
Coire
Cas

Glenmore Lodge

Youth Hostel

Finish

Loch Morlich

ROTHIEMURCHUS
FOREST

N

Coylumbridge
Start

B 970

To
Inverdruie
& Aviemore

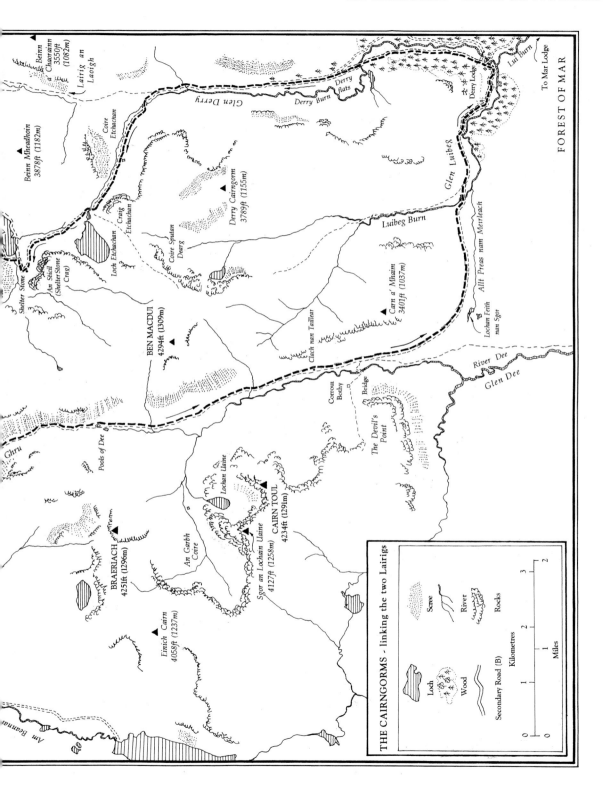

Beinn a' Chaorainn
3550ft (1082m)

Lairig an Laoigh

Beinn Mheadhoin
3878ft (1182m)

Coire Etchachan

Glen Derry

Derry Burn

Derry flats

Derry Lodge

Lui Burn

To Mar Lodge

FOREST OF MAR

Glen Luibeg

Craig Etchachan

Loch Etchachan

Coire Sputan Dearg

Derry Cairngorm
3789ft (1155m)

Luibeg Burn

Allt Preas nam Meirleach

Shelter Stone

An Sticil (Shelter Stone Crag)

BEN MACDUI
4294ft (1309m)

Carn a' Mhaim
3401ft (1037m)

Lochan Feith nan Sgor

Clach nan Taillear

Ghru

Pools of Dee

Corrour Bothy

Bridge

River Dee

Glen Dee

The Devil's Point

BRAERIACH
4251ft (1296m)

An Garbh Coire

Lochan Uaine

Sgor an Lochain Uaine
4127ft (1258m)

CAIRN TOUL
4234ft (1291m)

Einich Cairn
4058ft (1237m)

Am Beannac

THE CAIRNGORMS - linking the two Lairigs

Loch

Scree

Wood

River

Secondary Road (B)

Rocks

Kilometres
0 1 2 3

Miles
0 1 2

life tumbles down from the high Braeriach plateau into the An Gharbh Coire and subsequently down the length of the Lairig Ghru, and the Derry Burn, which is born in the high Arctic cirque of Coire Etchachan and flows down into Glen Derry, where it meets up with the Luibeg Burn to form the Lui Water, before merging with the Dee a short distance east of the Linn o' Dee.

Both these watercourses are still re-shaping two of the major *mounths*, or passes, of the Cairngorms: the Lairig Ghru, an historical through-route from Aviemore on the River Spey in the north to Braemar in the south, and the Lairig an Laoigh, which connects Abernethy in the north with Braemar in the south. Both passes once upon a time resounded to the movement of cattle: Lairig an Laoigh is 'the pass of stirks', or 'calves', and it's said that the older beasts were driven over the tougher, less forgiving terrain of the Lairig Ghru. Not only did the steep walls of both passes echo to the cacophony of herded cattle but also to human voices and the cry of tragedy. Caterans, thieves and robbers knew both routes intimately, good routes avoiding centres of population, and armies marched over them too, traversing the high passes God knows how many times on their ceaseless marches during their ceaseless wars. Despite the grand commanders, the dukes, marquises, knights and princes, it is the common cateran who has left his mark. History has chosen to commemorate the vagabonds and thieves by such place-names as Allt Preas nam Meirleach – 'the Stream of the Thieves' Bush' and Cnapan nam Meirleach – 'the Small Knoll of the Thieves'. A pair of drunken tailors are remembered in the Lairig Ghru; the Clach nan Taillear is the name of the rock where they tried to shelter from a storm one Hogmanay, New Year's Eve, many decades ago after trying to negotiate the winter Lairig after a night of merrymaking in Abernethy and Inverdruie.

A particularly fine excursion around the central massif of the Cairngorms can be experienced by linking the two main passes, the Lairig Ghru and the Lairig an Laoigh, starting at Coylumbridge near Aviemore and finishing at Glenmore Lodge in Glenmore near Loch Morlich, a distance of some 40 miles (64 km). All the route is on good tracks, but this is no mere low-level alternative to tramping the high tops of the Cairngorms. The Lairig Ghru rises to a height of 2733 feet (833 m), and both passes can become blocked by deep, drifting snow even in June. I've experienced falling snow in every month of the year in the Cairngorms. But with careful planning and one ear cocked towards the weather forecast, a linked traverse of both Lairigs is not only a superb introduction to the glories of the Cairngorms but a fabulous two- to three-day expedition through some of the wildest country Scotland has to offer. It's a trip that also gives an insight into some of the reasons why the Cairngorms could be one of Scotland's first National Parks.

Whenever one thinks of conservation and the ongoing battle of will between environmentalists and developers, the Cairngorms inevitably come to mind. There are a number of reasons for this. The Cairngorms present a huge mountainous area of prime conservation value, boasting the largest mass of uninhabited upland at over 2000, 3000 and 4000 feet (610, 914 and 1220 m) in the country, an area that provides habitats for species which are not found in any great number anywhere else, largely because the Cairngorms is the most southern of that land type we would call Arctic.

Secondly, the area, including the remnants of the pine forest of Caledon which skirt its flanks, is incredibly beautiful and attracts many people whose sole recreation is the appreciation and enjoyment of looking at and being within touching distance of natural beauty. In addition to these tourists are the walkers, the climbers, the moun-tain-bikers and the skiers, all with an equal justification for being there, utilizing nat-ural landscape for the enjoyment, and in some cases development, of their sport. Although it was popular in the past, the traditional country sports of deerstalking and grouse-shooting are not as widespread in the Cairngorms today as they were once, although they still take place on the fringes.

In short the Cairngorms, one of the most attractive and unusual landscapes in the country, attracts people in great numbers, and that basically is the problem. Of all the visitors, the skiers have wrought the greatest damage to date. The physical develop-ment of Coire Cas and Coire na Ciste, the main Cairngorm ski areas, to create the necessary infrastructure for downhill skiing has been tremendous, and it's now evident that much secondary damage has been done to the landscape by the access that's been created by the simple presence of a high-level car park and a chairlift that will take you to the top of Cairngorm. The replacement of the ageing chairlift by a funicular train, which at the time of writing looks increasingly likely, is largely unimportant – the issue is how many more people will that train carry to the top of Cairngorm and the adjoin-ing Cairngorm plateau, where the landscape is extremely sensitive to the pressures of large numbers of trampling feet?

My own conservation ethic is a simple one. We are but part of an intricate web of creation, of life, a web that in its design is finely tuned and finely balanced. Our prob-lems begin when we consider man to be the owner and user (and ultimately the abuser) of that web, and that everything else exists simply for our use, an anthropocen-tric view that derives from our Western Judaeo-Christian heritage that claims that man has been given dominance over the beasts of the land, the fish of the sea and every living thing. Unfortunately, our early Church fathers, through ignorance, greed or perhaps political gain, interpreted that as man being in dominance and dominating everything on earth. How much more rewarding it is to consider the root of that word 'dominion' as *dominus*, the caretaker of the house. Only then can we understand the wise words of the noted American ecologist Aldo Leopold: 'We abuse the land because we regard it as a community belonging to us. When we see the land as a community to which we belong, we may begin to use it with love and respect.'

It is with that understanding that I go into areas like the Cairngorms; to be a part of it, to accept it in its natural state, and in doing so I am more often than not given a sense of belonging, a oneness with the landscape which refreshes me, inspires me, motivates me and often heals me.

Above: The deep chasm of the Lairig Ghru from Sron na Lairige

Right: Rothiemurchus Forest, one of the finest
remnants of the ancient forest of Caledon

•

Coylumbridge to Derry Lodge

The Rothiemurchus Forest is an area that has probably changed little in several hundred years and yet conservation action has halted a steady decline in its main endearing feature, the pines, junipers and associated wildlife of the ancient Caledonian Pine Forest. The Lairig Ghru trail, which leaves the B970 Aviemore to Glenmore road at Coylumbridge, thrusts you into the forest without preamble. Scots pines, the patriarchs of the forest, line the pathside to welcome you. Birch trees grow in extravagant excess, juniper bushes cover the floor, and a rich, luxuriant undergrowth of heather, blaeberry and mosses gives an impression of timelessness. However, it wasn't so long ago that wild beasts like wolves, bears, elk and lynx roamed through this forest, avoiding the man-beast who was to hunt them to extinction. Later much of this great forest was cleared for timber, and we lost those remaining species that had made this thick woodland their home. We upset the balance of nature, broke the fine web, and only now are we realizing the consequences of doing so.

Ecologists have suggested that because of our largely unthinking actions we lose one species of flora or fauna worldwide every hour. If that's not serious enough, our actions are having sombre effects on other parts of the earth's fabric. For example, here was I, on a day in early February enjoying unseasonally warm sunshine. Nothing odd in that, and extremely pleasant, but I passed an alder that was almost bursting into bud. The sight of it pulled me up short, and I stared at it with disbelieving eyes – buds on branches on a tree which, in these northern latitudes, shouldn't be evident until late March at the earliest? The high tops beyond the topmost pines were pockmarked with the remnants of snow fields – at that time of the year the tops should be swathed in snow, but there hasn't been a proper winter, whatever that is, in ten years.

I've recently watched film of ice shelves on Arctic glaciers peeling off and falling into the sea. Scientists reckon that the icecaps are succumbing slowly to the sun's intensity through a depleted ozone layer and that this will affect the temperature of the sea, which will in turn affect the course of the Gulf Stream, which will in turn affect the climate, which will in turn affect us, possibly in ways that could yet prove to be devastating. The earth's natural balance has been upset, and things go out of kilter, possibly seriously. And while our carbon fuel emissions manifest in global warming, and has global significance, whatever we do at a local level will, ultimately, have a local significance.

We can allow 50 000 pairs of boots a year to tread a line between the top station of a funicular railway and the Cairngorm plateau, but the damage done by that line of trampling boots not only destroys the grasses and the lichens and the mosses but also the insects that live on the grasses, lichens and mosses, which in turn affect the birds that live on the insects, and so on – a chain reaction.

I followed the trail up through the forest alongside the roaring waters of the Am Beannaidh. Beyond the forest crossroads known as Piccadilly, the trail began to climb gently. Now the trees were becoming noticeably smaller, miniatures of their downhill relatives. I love these trees. They represent the spirit of Rothiemurchus, the spirit of the Caledonian Pine Forest. As I broke free of the forest, I stopped to look back to where I had come from. Like a green ocean, the treetops flowed northwards to lap gently on the foothills of the Monadhliath mountains on the other side of Strathspey. Am Monadh Liath are the grey hills, while the Cairngorms are more correctly named Am Monadh Ruadh, the red hills. 'Cairngorms' is a fairly recent name, and as you turn to resume your hike towards the jawed portals of the Lairig Ghru, and if you're there as the sun is beginning to sink, you'll understand why they were called the red hills. The lowering sun intensifies the pink colour of the dominant granite rock of the open hill-sides with a luminous glow, a warmth that is inviting. But this wasn't a warm summer evening, and the open jaws of the Lairig Ghru beckoned this walker from the benevolent forest into a very different world.

As the steep sides of the pass began to press in, I was suddenly aware that I had entered a true Arctic environment where life is sustained by slimmer threads. Can this cold world be called wilderness? In his book *Wilderness and the American Mind*, Roderick Nash suggests:

> *The usual dictionary sense of wilderness implies hostility in Man's part, but the term has also developed a favourable connotation. Although English dictionaries avoid the dual meaning, the chief German work on the subject confronts it directly. According to Jacob and Wilhelm Grimm and their revisers, Wildnis has a twofold emotional tone. On the one hand it is inhospitable, alien, mysterious and threatening: on the other hand beautiful, friendly and capable of elevating and delighting the beholder. Involved too in this second conception is the value of wild country as a sanctuary in which those in need of consolation can find respite from the pressures of civilization.*

I wonder if there can be a conjoining of these two aspects of wilderness? There's something in its attraction which brings together the sensations of mystery and tacit threat with the more acceptable beauty and sanctity. There's a challenge in its apparent malevolence, an attraction in its wildness which somehow makes it more worthy. A flower-filled meadow is beautiful and friendly and is capable of filling me with sheer delight, but it lacks the cutting, bracing edge that adds harshness to the primordial beauty of the hills. Such an edge, more often than not, suggests challenge, and challenge usually contains an element of doubt, of uncertainty, probably best summed up as risk.

Any winter crossing of the Lairig Ghru contains an element of risk. The pass rises only to 2733 feet (833 m) in height, but the summit of the Lairig often takes people by surprise: it's a boulder-strewn defile which can often act as a wind funnel, blowing snow

In the lower flats of Glen Derry at the southern end of the Lairig an Laoigh

into contorted and confusing shapes. Today, a light covering of snow made the boulders a slippery obstacle, and I was glad to have the reassurance of my two trekking poles for added support and balance. In any conditions there is usually an unspoken relief in crossing the summit of the Lairig Ghru, passing the Pools of Dee, four saucers of water held in the cusp of the pass, and starting the descent into Glen Dee, towards easier ground.

Soon after the summit, the narrow confines of the pass begin to widen out again and one of Scotland's finest corries begins to display itself on the right. This is An Gharbh Coire, 'the Big Rough Corrie', a great wild scooped-out hollow which bites hungrily into three Munros: Braeriach, Sgor an Lochain Uaine and Cairn Toul. This huge corrie is one of the great features of the Cairngorms and I would rank it among the top three corries in Scotland along with Coire Mhic Fhearchair of Beinn Eighe and Toll an Lochan of An Teallach. High up on its south-west flanks lies a great patch of snow which is the closest we have in Scotland to a glacier. It's completely vanished only a handful of times this century, up until five years ago that is. In the past five years it's melted every year – which gives an idea of how our weather patterns are changing.

The path is soon joined by the infant waters of the River Dee. Although still young (its source is high on the Braeriach plateau), it has already grown fairly wide, and a bridge crosses it further downstream near Corrour Bothy, a bridge which is not without its critics. I had now crossed onto land owned by the National Trust for Scotland. This Mar Lodge Estate was sold to the Trust in 1995 and they are currently examining the whole question of man-made structures on the estate. Corrour Bothy, an old deer-watcher's house, nestles below the black flanks of The Devil's Point on the opposite side of the Dee from the Lairig Ghru footpath, and a bridge was constructed some years ago across to it. Unfortunately, the bridge has concentrated people onto the same route, and tremendous erosion has occurred on the peaty ground between the bridge and the bothy. Some would suggest that such man-made structures should have no place in a wild area like the Cairngorms, and the Cairngorms Partnership, a talking shop set up by Scottish Natural Heritage to work out a strategy plan for the future of the Cairngorms, recommends the removal of all such structures within the area.

It struck me as I strode down the path opposite the bothy that although one of the problems the bothy faces was that of too many people using it, I hadn't seen a soul all day. The Lairig in winter is a different beast from the popular route it is in the summer. One of the main problems is that daylight tends to be in short supply in winter, and already I was aware that I didn't have much of it left. I wanted to camp for the night at Derry Lodge, a disused shooting-lodge where there are some delightful camping spots below the pines, but that was still some way off. With darkness falling before six o'clock, I knew I'd have a good hour or so to walk by the light of my headtorch, but that didn't worry me too much. A good track runs down Glen Luibeg, past the old stalkers' house, all the way to the pines of Derry Lodge itself.

Where the track rounds the shoulder of Carn a' Mhaim the view for the first time opens towards the east and on the horizon lie the peaks of Lochnagar and the Balmoral forest. I passed the ruffled waters of Lochan Feith nan Sgor, appropriately the Lochan of Bog of the Rocky Hills, and dropped down to cross the Luibeg Burn in the growing darkness. To the south, up the length of Glen Luibeg, I could just discern the vertical cliffs of Coire Sputan Dearg and, high above them, the first evening star.

The National Trust for Scotland doesn't appear to be very sure what they are going to do with Derry Lodge. It's been suggested that it would make a good bunkhouse, or private hostel; others have suggested it should simply be pulled down. I'm not sure what the answer is; the building has been there for such a long time it's almost become part of the landscape, and I would have thought it would make a wonderful hostel. The only slight problem is that the Trust might then ban camping, which would be a pity because the surrounding area offers one of the finest camping spots in the Cairngorms. Close by where the Lui and Derry Burns meet, beneath some very old and gnarled Scots pines, are some green, grassy swards, just made for pitching a lightweight tent. My wife and I used to bring our eldest son here when he was a toddler. At that time we were wardens of Aberdeen Youth Hostel and now and again, when we could escape, we used to come here for a welcome break, usually just overnight. The huge attraction for Gordon was the number of red deer stags that would come and graze around the tent. They seemed totally unperturbed by the delighted cries of an 18-month-old child.

Darkness had fallen by the time I arrived at my favourite spot below the pines and the well-rehearsed routine came into play. I slipped the pack from my shoulders with a grunt of relief. The first item out was the tent bag, and within five minutes or so I had a welcome refuge. Twenty minutes later I was lying on my side in a well-fluffed-out sleeping-bag watching water boil on the stove in anticipation of a good meal, a dram and a long, peaceful night. One of the great attractions of wilderness walking is that you can go to bed at eight-thirty without people thinking you're either antisocial or ill!

Derry Lodge to Loch Avon

The Lairig an Laoigh runs south from Abernethy Forest, east of Bynack More, over the River Avon at Fords of Avon, where legend claims the wife of the semi-mythological warrior Fionn MacCumhail (Fingal) was swept away to her death, and down the length of Glen Derry between the giant peaks of Beinn Mheadhoin and Derry Cairngorm on one side and Beinn a' Chaorainn and Beinn Bhreac on the other. Like the Lairig Ghru it's an ancient north–south route, but unlike the Lairig Ghru it's comparatively devoid of walkers.

An arctic scene: Loch Etchachan from Stacan Dubha

•

From Derry Lodge an old footpath runs through more remnants of the ancient pine forest before meeting the bulldozed track that runs north through the Derry flats. It's a pleasant enough walk but lacks the rugged grandeur of its twin pass, the Lairig Ghru. With the weather remaining unseasonally mild, and surprisingly settled, I decided to take a little diversion into the very heartland of these central Cairngorms, up the length of Coire Etchachan to Loch Etchachan, possibly my favourite spot in these high Cairngorms, before dropping down to the cathedral-like grandeur of the head of Loch Avon. A walk along the shoreline to The Saddle at the head of Strath Nethy would give a good start to my third day before heading for home down Strath Nethy to Bynack Stable, Ryvoan Pass and back to the B970 at Loch Morlich past Glenmore Lodge, where a pint of beer would make a pleasant reward for my endeavours.

The track up Coire Etchachan gives a good foretaste of things to come. Passing the small Hutchison Memorial Hut, one of the less obtrusive and controversial of the Cairngorm bothies, the pass strikes steeply uphill, a well-used and considerably eroded footpath that is calling out for regular maintenance work. It's a trail used by walkers and climbers alike, for the cliffs of Craig Etchachan and, more important, the Sticil crag above the Shelter Stone at the head of Loch Avon are both popular and challenging. This is a track where you're more likely to hear the broad vowels of the Aberdonian dialect than anything else, the Aberdeen school being an erstwhile *tour de force* of Scottish mountaineering.

As I pushed on up the path, delighting in the large patches of glistening snow hanging like curtains from the crags, I considered the whole question of footpath maintenance. Who should pay for it? Who should take responsibility for it? Here the National Trust for Scotland has initiated an ambitious programme of maintenance, well aware that such work is not only making footpaths less obtrusive but in fact performs a healing process on the landscape. Paths become severely eroded when they become watercourses, not an unusual occurrence in our climate, but when watercourses occur walkers tend to walk to the side of it, so producing another footpath, and another potential watercourse. It doesn't take long for footpaths to become several yards wide. Footpath maintenance adds drainage structures and puts in place some sort of solid footing, usually a form of stone cobbling, so that walkers are encouraged to walk on the actual path. When this happens, plants and grasses at the side of the path can grow quickly over the old scarring and so the landscape effectively is repaired.

Loch Etchachan is the most Arctic-like feature of these Arctic Cairngorms. Caressing the 3000-foot (914-m) contour, it fills the high corrie which is held in the cusp of Ben Macdui, Beinn Mheadhoin and Derry Cairngorm. I've camped here many times, and often I've thought I could have been sharing a sward with polar bears in northern Greenland or awaiting the howling of huskies on Baffin Island. In winters past this high-level tarn would have been frozen solid for all but three or four months of the year, but nowadays things are different: it was completely clear of ice!

There's something about these high-level slopes just east of Ben Macdui which enthrals me and draws me back time after time. The attraction is in the wide-open skies, the opportunity to stroll over glaciated slopes for hours on end and never drop below the 3000-foot (914-m) contour – the rare privilege of being able to walk on the roof of Scotland. I stopped for a while after the long pull out of Coire Etchachan. A flock of snow buntings cavorted close by, and in the distance, somewhere across the loch, a ptarmigan grunted its distinctive cry. The unseasonal mildness had made me feel rather lazy, and I lay back among some rocks and pondered the future of the Cairngorms as a National Park.

The creation of at least two National Parks, one covering the Trossachs and Loch Lomond area and the other in the Cairngorms, looks likely to be established early in the next century, the child of the proposed Scottish Parliament. But I am yet to be convinced that National Parks, as they exist in England and Wales or North America, are the answer here in Scotland. I'm suspicious of the break-up of a fine and grand whole – which is the entire Highlands and Islands – into smaller fragments. How can anyone suggest that the Cairngorms or Loch Lomond are more deserving of National Park status than Torridon or Letterewe or the Cuillins or the stupendous limestone landscape of Inchnadamph in the far north-west? Is there not an argument in Scotland for the entire Highlands and Islands to be given a unique Scottish form of National Park status and so assure the future of not only the flora and fauna but also a culture and the Gaelic language? This could well be a first, a first for a nascent Scottish Parliament in the world of landscape and cultural conservation, but the power of landowning interests in Scotland is such that an original scheme of this nature is highly unlikely.

Just as the high-level wastes give way to the lower elevations of Loch Etchachan, so Loch Etchachan and its surrounding gravelly slopes give way to Loch Avon. Set in its high trench between Cairngorm itself and the tor-studded slopes of Beinn Mheadhoin, Loch Avon is the jewel of the Cairngorms, the heart of this landscape of landscapes, a masterpiece in this land of grandeur. Its headwaters all but lap the vertical stone of An Sticil (generally known as the Shelter Stone Crag), a mind-blowing chunk of rock no less than 800 feet (240 m) in height, a square block of Cyclopean granite that jars all preconceived notions of the Cairngorms being an area of swelling, breasted hills, however big. Here is rock architecture at its most brazen, cliff scenery at its most audacious. I've often sat on top of this awesome block, perched on its sheer, vertical edge, looking down at the jumble of boulders and blocks at its feet and felt small and unimportant, but standing at its bottom looking up, however foreshortened it may appear, is a humbling experience, and I felt the insignificance of my human nature once again when arrayed against the comparatively timeless and enduring nature of such wonder.

I camped within a stone's throw of An Sticil, positioning my tent so that I could look out and see it. Deep within its boulder-strewn skirts lay the Shelter Stone itself, a

MORNING MISTS IN THE PASS OF RYVOAN

•

huge granite boulder tilted at such an angle that it forms the roof of a natural cave big enough for several people to sleep in side by side. Its history is significant. Once the lair of robbers and vagabonds, it gained some respectability when Prime Minister Gladstone stayed in it during a hill-walking expedition. More recently, it has sheltered Prince Charles, an enthusiast for these Cairngorm mountains. I eased off to sleep thinking that its future as a shelter was far more assured than any man-made bothy.

Loch Avon to Glenmore Lodge

A number of footpaths trace their way along the northern shore of Loch Avon, the widest of them leaving the shoreline after a few hundred yards to climb into the steep defile of Coire Raibeirt, where a steep line can be climbed onto the Cairngorm plateau just south-west of Cairngorm itself. My route stayed by the rocky water margins, where small waves left a white scum mark contrasting vividly with the aquamarine blue of the loch. Black-headed gulls wheeled above the waters, and I spent some time gazing at peregrine-haunted crags. Even at these relatively lower elevations ptarmigan still croaked their defiance, their white-feathered camouflage ironically casting them vivid against the unseasonally snowless rocks.

The path soon began to rise beyond the waters of Loch Avon and onto The Saddle, the col between Cairngorm and the south-western slopes of A' Chòinneach. From here a long and narrow glen, Strath Nethy, flowed north towards Abernethy Forest and Ryvoan, where I would find the bulldozed track that would take me through the Pass of Ryvoan and its Lochan Uaine, the Green Lochan, so tainted because the fairy people traditionally wash their clothes here. From there it would be only a mile or so to Glenmore Lodge and its public bar, where I would enjoy a pint of beer before phoning for a taxi to run me the three miles (five km) or so back to my starting-point at Coylumbridge.

As I trod down the long miles of Strath Nethy, deep within the RSPB's Abernethy reserve, I was thankful that at least the Cairngorms are enjoying a measure of protection. The RSPB own a large part of this area, the National Trust for Scotland own Mar Lodge, Rothiemurchus Estate is owned by the Grant family who manage the estate on conservation principles; but surely an area of such international significance shouldn't have to depend on voluntary bodies or the good nature of a private family for protection? Such protection is surely a governmental responsibility. Maybe we have to tempt our politicians into areas like the Cairngorms and allow the landscape to speak for itself.

CHAPTER SIX

FLOWERDALE

THE HILLS OF TIME

•

Cameron McNeish

A two-day walk over the Torridonian hills of Beinn an Eòin, Beinn Dearg and Baosbheinn

---

MAP: *OS 1:50 000 Sheet 19*
START AND FINISH: *Beside Am Feur Loch on the A832 Loch Maree to Gairloch road. Grid Ref: 857721*
LENGTH: *About 25 miles (40 km)*
APPROXIMATE TIME: *2 days*
TERRAIN: *Mostly on rough, trackless mountain terrain. Some scrambling involved on Beinn Dearg*
ACCOMMODATION: *Hotels and b&bs in Kinlochewe and Gairloch, youth hostel and campsite at Torridon*

I t's easy to be fooled by names. The Flowerdale Forest, in Ross-shire in the north-west of Scotland, sounds as though it should be a gentle, idyllic sort of a place. The term 'dale' has about it a softness, a suggestion of pastoral delight, and evokes less harsh imagery than the Scottish word 'glen'. That this area is called a forest also suggests a sheltering, a protection from the more usual Ross-shire weather of rain and wind.

But this is not a forest in the literal sense. Flowerdale is a traditional deer-shooting estate and is termed a deer forest, a rather misleading description since trees are few and far between. And there is little soft or pastoral about Flowerdale: this wild area, forming the northern boundaries of what we call Torridon, is a harsh and unforgiving land of mountain and flood, the innumerable lochs and lochans of its hinterland giving hint of a great watery moorland where footpaths are notable by their absence, a place where the steep-sided mountains dominate the eye, the mind and the spirit.

Three peaks in particular rise sheer from the watery mosaic that forms their plinth: Baosbheinn (2871 feet/875 m), Beinn an Eòin (2805 feet/855 m) and Beinn Dearg (2998 feet/914 m). The first two face each other across the waters of Loch na h-Oidhche. Both are long and linear, with narrow ridges linking the main summits,

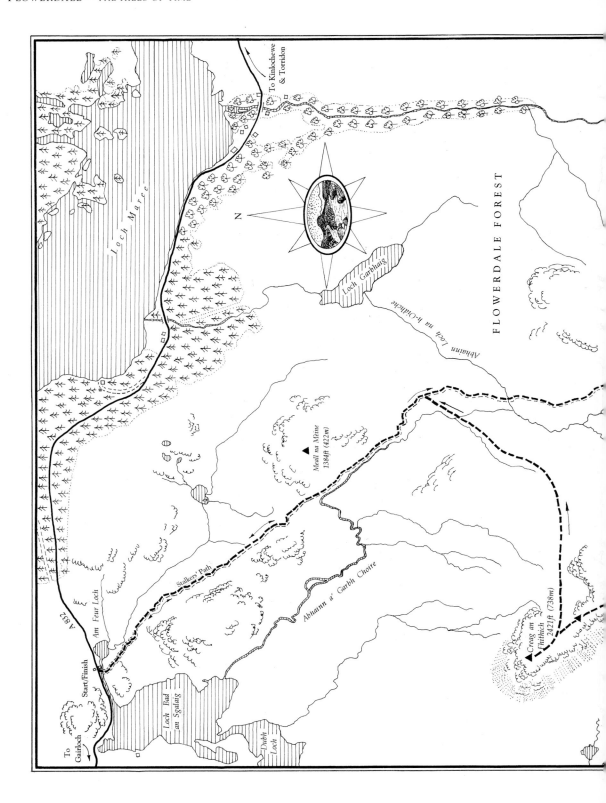

To Kinlochewe
& Torridon

Loch Maree

FLOWERDALE FOREST

N

Loch Garbhaig

Abhainn Loch na h-Oidhche

Meall na Mèine
1384ft (422m)

Stalkers' Path

Abhainn a' Garbh Choire

Creag an
Fhithich
2421ft (738m)

A832

Am Feur Loch

Start/Finish

To
Gairloch

Loch Bad
an Sgalaig

Dubh
Loch

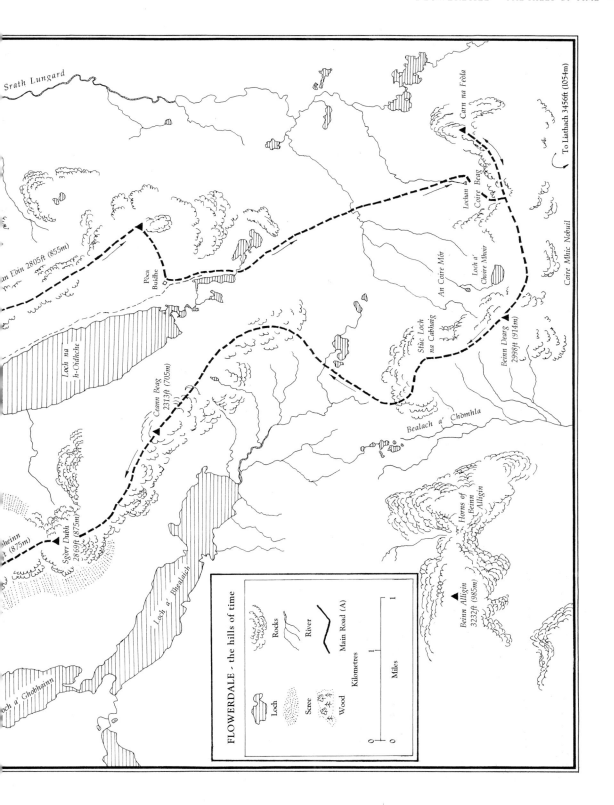

Srath Lungard

an Eòin 2805ft (855m)

Pòca
Buidhe

Loch na
h-Oidhche

Ceann Beag
2313ft (705m)

Loch a' Bhealaich

heinn
t (875m)

Sgòrr Dubh
2869ft (875m)

och a' Ghobhainn

Carn na Fèola

To Liathach 3456ft (1054m)

Lochan
Coire Beag

An Coire Mòr

Loch a'
Choire Mhoir

Coire Mhic Nobuil

Stùc Loch
na Cabhaig

Beinn Dearg
2998ft (914m)

Bealach a' Chòmhla

Horns of
Beinn
Alligin

Beinn Alligin
3232ft (985m)

FLOWERDALE - the hills of time

Loch

Scree

Wood

Kilometres

Miles

Rocks

River

Main Road (A)

while further south Beinn Dearg is horseshoe-shaped, its enclosing ramparts clutching two fine north-facing corries, An Coire Mór and Coire Beag. A traverse of all three mountains, from the A832 Loch Maree to Gairloch road in the north, offers a great two-day mountain-horseshoe route of some 25 miles (40 km), maybe not far in terms of distance but a substantially tough trip, climbing some of the oldest mountains in the world.

These mountains of Torridon were raised as a vast plateau 30 million years ago and subsequently were carved into their present shape. The rock of the original chain, now exposed as the mountain's quartzite caps, is reckoned to be 600 million years old. The sandstone below them is even older, and the platforms of gneiss on which they stand are believed to be somewhere in the region of 2600 million years old. This gneiss is certainly among the oldest rocks in the Highlands, and indeed everywhere on earth the oldest known rocks are gneisses. This Highland gneiss is pink or grey, of both igneous and sedimentary origin, which has been toughened by heat and pressure deep in the earth. It's thought to underlie all Highland rock – indeed, it's thought to cover a huge geographical area, from the Urals of Russia, through Greenland and across Canada.

It's been said that geology is the womb of history. For the last hour or so I had driven past some of the most astonishing landscape in the UK: the leviathan shape of Liathach, the magnificent quartzite-capped peaks and pinnacles of Beinn Eighe and the castle-like ramparts of Slioch across the waters of Loch Maree. Now, with the car safely parked for a couple of days near the white corrugated-iron barn beside the A832 and my pack heaved on my back, I had the time and space to try to think through this whole amazing concept of geological history and beyond, to fundamental questions which lay their basis at the door of the greatest question of all – where and when did life begin?

A stalkers' path begins on the opposite side of the road, just beyond the outflow of the lovely Am Feur Loch. Gulls wheeled above the loch and skylarks filled the warm air with their enthusiastic song. White bog cotton carpeted the surrounding moorland, ruffled gently by the merest breath of air. These Flowerdale Forest peaks are not the easiest hills to climb. Miles of rock-strewn, boggy moorland protect them from car-borne mountain-baggers; this stalkers' path, running in for almost four miles (six km) from the road to a boat-house at the northern end of Loch na h-Oidhche, is one of the very few lines of least resistance. From there onwards, walkers and backpackers must take to the trackless heather.

The landscape became increasingly wild as I walked south, a gentle introduction to Flowerdale that allowed limbs to ease themselves slowly into the wilderness. Within minutes I felt overdressed in shorts and T-shirt, but it was comforting to hear the reassuring creak of my pack harness and the gentle click-click of trekking poles on the hard-packed footpath. Within the first mile the path entered a narrow defile and welcome shade before climbing gradually to meet the Abhainn a' Garbh Choire below the western rocky slopes of Meall na Mèine. Ahead I caught the first glimpse of Baosbheinn's row of peaks, but my first peak, Beinn an Eòin, still hid itself shyly behind Meall na Mèine, 'the mossy peak'.

Soon Beinn an Eòin came into view, but before I could get to grips with its steep slopes I had to cross the Abhainn Loch na h-Oidhche, the river that flows out of its eponymous loch. Fortunately, the water-level was low, the result of a snowless winter and a dry spring, and I managed to cross virtually dryshod. After two hours of relaxed walking I reached the northern shores of Loch na h-Oidhche and took shelter from the sun in the squat boat-house. It was time for a long, cold drink and a survey down the length of the loch towards the big hills that burst through the earth's crust like sandstone skeletons.

My understanding of geology is sketchy in the extreme, but I was aware that I couldn't begin to understand any of its complexities until I had grasped some sort of meaning about time itself. Ralph Waldo Emerson once wrote: 'There is a relation between the hours of our life and the centuries of time. The hours should be instructed by the ages, and the ages explained by the hours.'

My problem was one that is probably shared by many geological laymen. I had the distinct tendency – some may call it conceit – to regard the majestically slow processes of geological time as a mere prelude to the comparatively short and turbulent history of mankind. And yet I was aware enough to realize that the sum total of man's activity on the planet was no more than the flicker of an eye. We are but comparatively recent visitors, and, if we are to believe the most pessimistic of the environmentalists, our tenure may well be short lived. But philosophy would have us look at the whole question of time and creation through different eyes. The unfolding of life's drama on the earth has seen a slow but steady evolution from lower to higher life forms, ultimately producing a race of beings with a higher intellect, apparently, than any other living creature. Is there a philosophical argument, then, which suggests that mere time is not the proper yardstick of assessment, but this slow and gradual evolution has been no more than an unhurried preparation for the emergence of the human race?

I'm aware that this is a very man-centred view which suggests that the world revolves around *Homo sapiens* and his doings, but there is a risk that opposing views condemn us to a mechanistic conception of life. By taking such opposing views we tend to regard man's achievements as mere 'chance', and our moral and ethical purposes quickly become quenched in the flames of a future extinction. On the other hand, the archives of the rocks offer optimism, particularly when we look at the small print which explains something of this spinning rock we call the earth.

The steep scramble up to the Beinn an Eòin ridge took all my attention, geological optimism temporarily set aside as I wallowed in a lather of sweat up 1000 feet (305 m) of rock and grass to reach the final fringe of weathered sandstone outcrops. Unlike some of their higher neighbours, these hills of Flowerdale have long lost their quartzite

ABOVE: THE FOOTPATH TO LOCH NA H-OIDHCHE

RIGHT: SUNSET OVER THE FLOWERDALE PEAKS OF BAOSBHEINN AND BEINN AN EÒIN FROM BEINN EIGHE

caps and protrude from their gneiss bedrock like rows of toothless gums. Although the rocks provided some shelter from the excesses of the August sun, I couldn't help but gaze down below me on the still waters of Loch na h-Oidhche, 'the Loch of Night'. The name probably reflects the benefits of the loch for its night-time fishing, a pastime that suddenly seemed sane and pleasant, drifting in an open boat with the cool of a night breeze keeping the midgies at bay.

Slightly cooler now, I pushed on to the broad scoured-sandstone ridge and saw it stretch onwards before me into the haze. Away on the northern horizon I could just discern the unmistakable castellated outline of An Teallach, and closer at hand, beyond Loch Garbhaig, an infinitely bigger stretch of island-studded water, Loch Maree, lapping against the oak-covered shores of Letterewe. The loch's islets and bays glinted green in the sun, almost matching the colour of the oak trees. At its far end Slioch brooded, fortress-like and impregnable, more like an ancient dun – a Pictish fort – than a mountain, wearing a halo of cloud like a crown.

The day wasn't one for rushing, and I would have been happy to sit there on the ridge and dream of mountains and lochs, but I wanted to reach Beinn Dearg by early evening. The plan was to camp as high as possible in the mountain's Coire Beag, where hopefully there would be water and a minimum of midgies. Time, that mis-understood and evocative notion, has an underhand way of continually playing against us, even in such glorious places. So often we escape one set of schedules and timetables only to impose another, completely different set.

Beinn an Eòin's ridge is generally fairly broad, and now that I felt a tad cooler I loped along it, enjoying the firm footing of mossy grass and sandstone slabs. After a mile or so of this delightful ridge-walking the slope ahead suddenly steepened and began to narrow appreciably. Almost subconsciously, I slowed down and scanned the slope ahead for the easiest line. I needn't have worried. As so often happens in hazy conditions, or in light mist, shapes look bigger or steeper than they are, and happily I followed pleasantly angled sandstone slabs all the way to the summit cairn, perched dramatically on a small plateau at the end of a four-foot-wide section of ridge. This, then, was Beinn an Eòin, 2805 feet (855 m), 'the Peak of the Bird'.

A quick run down rock-shattered slopes on the western side of the hill dropped me very rapidly to the cottage of Pòca Buidhe. It was locked. The stone-built bothy nestles naturally among some huge boulders, but it's easily betrayed by its red, rusting cor-rugated-iron roof. After my run down from Beinn an Eòin I was lathered again in sweat. A swim was a tempting proposition, but the midgies were already out and I was being bitten remorselessly by clegs. I wanted to keep moving.

Beinn Dearg lies two and a half miles (four km) south of Pòca Buidhe across a wilderness of weather-scoured sandstone slabs and boulders, quaking peat bogs and a landscape that would appear to contain more pools, lochans and streams than dry land. With the biting insects I knew the journey could be desperately frustrating, but, with more good luck than skill, I managed to stumble across a well-placed series of glacier-scoured sandstone spines which avoided the worst of the bogs and pools. In just over 90 minutes I was clambering up slabs of rock beside a tiny lochan, deep in the bowels of Coire Beag of Beinn Dearg. Although I was higher than the loch-splattered moorland, clouds of midgies still darkened the prospects of a comfortable night, but I wasn't too worried. Once inside my tent I'd light a couple of green mosquito coils, place one at either side of my tent door, and cook supper in the tent's vestibule. I've used these mosquito coils for years and they've never let me down. Midgies and mosquitoes hate them, and I can enjoy an insect-free oasis in the middle of the most blood-sucking insect environments imaginable.

Supper over, I lay back in the tent and gazed through the open tent doors and the clouds of gently wafting smoke. The first stars were appearing, and I struggled to follow my thoughts of earlier, my appreciation of this sphere of rock and water we know as the earth. As far as my limited knowledge allows me to understand, the earth is uniquely suited to support life. It resides in a galaxy that has the right rate of supernova events to provide sufficient elements essential to life without life-destroying radiation. Incredibly, our sun is the right distance away from other stars in our galaxy to prevent gravitational interactions that would disrupt the orbits of the planets, yet still have an even distribution of the heavy elements necessary for life. Our sun also has the very specific mass that is necessary to maintain a temperature suitable for life on earth. The distance between the sun and the earth is appropriate to maintain the earth's current rotational rate. The distance between the sun and the earth is also what it must be to support the stability of liquid water, which is necessary for life to exist, but if the distance between the sun and the earth changed as little as two per cent, all life would cease to exist.

The moon, too, is as it must be to support life on the earth. It is unique in our solar system in that it is extraordinarily large in relation to its planet, earth. Its resulting gravitational pull stabilizes the tilt of the earth and also helps clean the waters of the seas and oceans and replenish their nutrients through the tidal cycle. It would appear, then, that the design of the universe, the galaxy, the solar system and our planet are just exactly as they must be to support life on the earth.

I gazed out of the tent into the dimming night. From somewhere close by came the chuckling of a ring ouzel and beyond the smoke a cloud of midgies hung in the air. Mountain shapes rose around me, and what light was left in the sky reflected off a million and one lochans and pools, glinting grey and metallic from the black moor. Could all this beauty and glory have come about simply by chance? A number of years ago the famous evolutionary Professor of Astronomy at Cambridge, Sir Fred Hoyle, made headlines in the nation's press. He had been trying to work out the possibility of life arising by chance and reached an interesting conclusion after detailed mathematical analysis of the belief that life could result from time, chance and the

TOP: LOCH NA H-OIDHCHE FROM BEINN AN EÒIN

ABOVE: THE SUMMIT RIDGE OF BAOSBHEINN LOOKING NORTH

properties of matter. It was, according to Sir Fred Hoyle, comparable to the belief that 'a tornado sweeping through a junkyard might assemble a Boeing 747 from the materials within'.

Beinn Dearg to Am Feur Loch

A fern-filled gully provided an easy route from Coire Beag to Carn na Feòla, the eastern summit of Beinn Dearg. There's a peculiar satisfaction about being on top of a mountain so early in the morning, and the immediate bonus was that the haze of yesterday had been dispelled by the cold night air. Here I was, perched on another immaculate mountain ridge gazing at one of Scotland's wildest mountains, Liathach.

From the south, in Glen Torridon, Liathach appears as a brooding giant, but from here, across the wide gulf of Coire Mhic Nobuil, her Am Fasarinen pinnacles and the deeply plunging cliffs and buttresses of Coire na Caime reveal another character, her darker side perhaps, underlining the complex topography of one of the most popular mountains among hill-walkers in the land.

Like Liathach, Beinn Dearg also has a surprisingly serious nature for walkers. Irvine Butterfield, in his excellent *The High Mountains of Britain and Ireland*, suggests that it's a mountain unsuitable for inexperienced parties in bad weather. The main difficulties are reached as you approach the main summit, at 2998 feet (914 m), where the ridge steepens and narrows considerably and sheer broken cliffs fall away into the depths of An Coire Mór. A rocky buttress appears to bar further progress, but this can be bypassed on the left by a very narrow footpath that appears to hang by its fingertips above the steep, broken chasms above Coire Mhic Nobuil. The exposure doesn't last for long, but I was almost sorry I hadn't tackled the rock buttress direct!

A few more rocky steps and I was on the flat summit of Beinn Dearg, almost overwhelmed by the magnificent views around me. To the west, across the Bealach a' Chòmhla, the impressive 'horns' of Beinn Alligin were grossly foreshortened by the angle but looked steep and forbidding none the less. Liathach was still arrayed in all her Torridonian splendour, and to the north-west the whaleback of Baosbheinn rose steeply above the blue waters of Loch a' Bhealaich. Suddenly, I was aware that I still had a long way to go.

The morning was well advanced as I carefully descended the steep and craggy western spur of Stùc Loch na Cabhaig, Beinn Dearg's northern top. A faint path zigzagged its way down the spur, avoiding the steepest sections, and I was for once grateful for signs of man's presence. An hour of bog-trotting took me north, and early afternoon saw me climbing through the sandstone formations on Ceann Beag, the southern summit of my final hill, Baosbheinn.

I sat and rested on a rocky platform, looking over and beyond Loch na h-Oidhche, and I realized for the first time, or I saw for the first time, that both Beinn an Eòin and Beinn Dearg were made up of strata upon strata of rock, horizontal layers mounted one on top of the other, exact replicas of the stratas that I was climbing on Baosbheinn. But I could now see clearly, as I moved my eye downhill, that the rocks were growing older, from the relatively young sandstone peaks, which once upon a time were probably graced by quartzite caps but which were now toothless, down through the aeons of time to the darker, older lower slopes and the bedrock of quantum-ancient gneiss. When sudden revelation visits us it comes with a dramatic crystal clarity that can be difficult to describe to others, and so it was with my sudden appreciation of the concept of geological time. Suddenly, I grasped it; I understood the mystery. More than anything else I realized that our clock and the geological clock keep different times. In a few hours I would be driving home to a hot shower, but in a few hours of geological time, where each hour might represent 10 000 years, the topmost sandstone strata on Beinn Dearg may well have worn away. I might still have lacked the explicit insight into the meaning of 600 million years, but I felt more at ease with the concept. What's more, I had a better understanding of the role that time had played in the creation of such harmony and beauty. The concept was actually quite simple: whoever or whatever had created this earth needed one thing more than anything else to design such magnificence – time!

Beinn Alligin and its horns rose menacingly across Loch a' Bhealaich as I climbed onwards, over Ceann Beag and along a broad, rounded ridge, then over two subsidiary summits to the final steep pull up to the hill's main summit, Sgòrr Dubh (2869 feet/ 875 m). A herd of red deer moved across the corrie floor below me as I walked on northwards to Creag an Fhithich, from where I could drop down the north-east slopes back to the rock-splattered moorland just north of Loch na h-Oidhche. Baosbheinn, 'the Wizard's Hill', had cast its spell on me, and I regained the path back to the road and my parked car well aware of the very simple miracle of Being.

Curiously, some words from a speech given by Václav Havel, the president of the Czech Republic, came to mind:

> *...the only real hope of people today is probably a renewal of our certainty that we are rooted in the earth, and at the same time in the cosmos. This awareness endows us with the capacity of self-transcendence.*

Self-transcendence – maybe that was the answer to the questions I'd been asking. It was later, when I reread the rest of Havel's speech, that I understood.

Politicians at international forums may reiterate a thousand times that the basis of the new world order must be universal respect for human rights, but it will mean nothing as long as this imperative does not derive from the respect of the miracle of being, the miracle of the Universe, the miracle of nature, the miracle of our own existence. Only someone who submits to the authority of the universal order and of creation, who values the right to be part of it and a participant in it, can genuinely value himself and his neighbours, and thus honour their rights as well. The Declaration of Independence states that the Creator gave man the right to liberty. It seems man can realize that liberty only if he does not forget the One who endowed him with it.

CHAPTER SEVEN

WINTER WALKING IN THE MONADHLIATH

NEGLECTED MOUNTAINS

●

Richard Else

A two-day winter exploration through these deserted mountains

---

MAP: *OS 1:50 000 Sheet 35*
START: *Garva Bridge. Grid Ref: 522948*
FINISH: *Newtonmore. Grid Ref: 714990*
LENGTH: *Almost 17 miles (27 km)*
APPROXIMATE TIME: *2 days in winter conditions*
TERRAIN: *Wild, featureless mountain country which requires careful navigation in bad weather. If attempting this trip in winter, a good level of fitness and experience is necessary together with the appropriate equipment and knowledge of how to use it*
ACCOMMODATION: *A variety of accommodation in both Newtonmore and Kingussie, including homely b&bs, friendly pubs and good hotels*

I have often wondered how many people, especially those living south of the border and whose trips to Scotland are usually no longer than limited holidays will allow, have ever explored the Monadhliath Mountains or even know exactly where they are situated. Munroists will have some appreciation of the region but often their exploration is limited to the four relevant hills in the area. In fact, finding a real champion of these hills is difficult, as they are often underrated by writers, who thus dismiss a huge area of upland bounded by the Corrieyairack Pass in

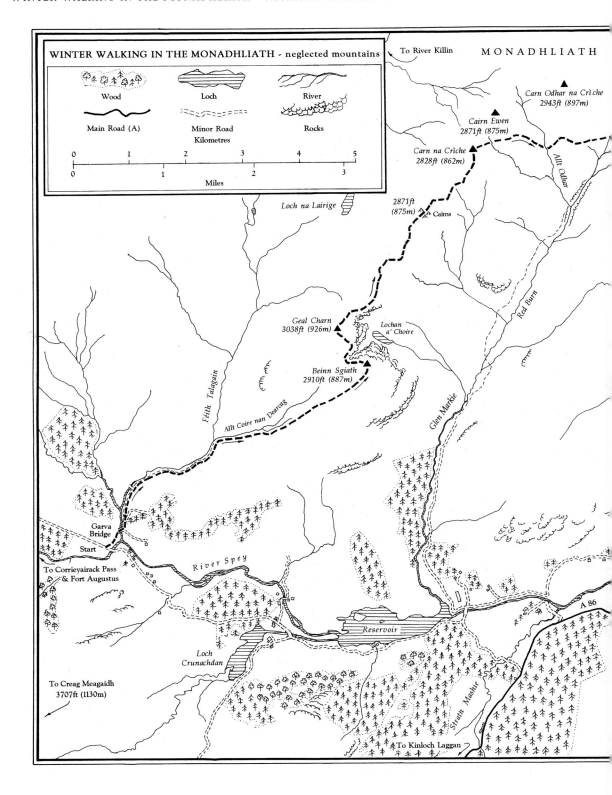

WINTER WALKING IN THE MONADHLIATH - neglected mountains

Wood   Loch   River

Main Road (A)   Minor Road   Rocks
Kilometres

To River Killin   MONADHLIATH

Carn Odhar na Crìche
2943ft (897m)

Cairn Ewen
2871ft (875m)

Carn na Crìche
2828ft (862m)

Allt Odhar

2871ft
(875m)   Cairns

Loch na Lairige

Red Burn

Geal Charn
3038ft (926m)   Lochan
a' Choire

Beinn Sgiath
2910ft (887m)

Glen Markie

Féith Talagain

Allt Coire nan Dearcag

Garva
Bridge

Start

To Corrieyairack Pass
& Fort Augustus

River Spey

Reservoir

A 86

Loch
Crunachdan

Strath Mashie

To Creag Meagaidh
3707ft (1130m)

To Kinloch Laggan

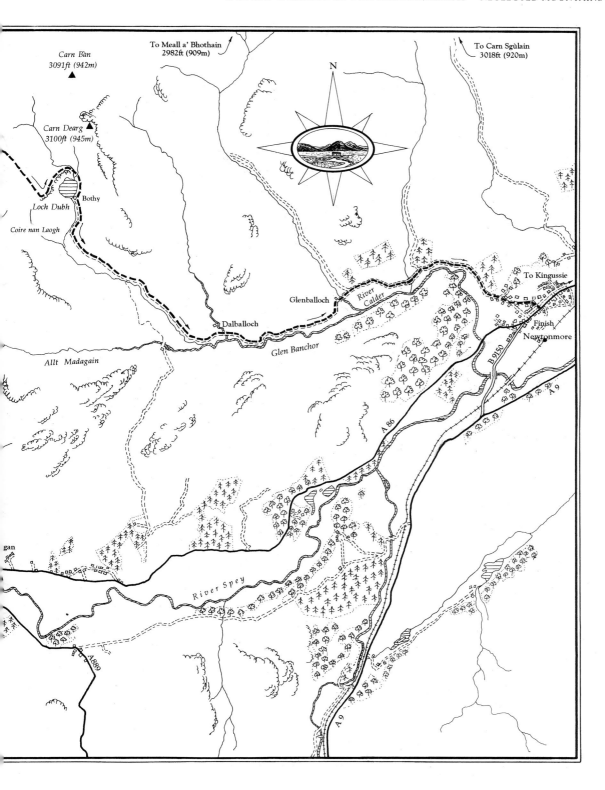

Carn Bàn
3091ft (942m)

To Meall a' Bhothain
2982ft (909m)

To Carn Sgùlain
3018ft (920m)

N

Carn Dearg
3100ft (945m)

Bothy

Loch Dubh

Coire nan Laogh

To Kingussie

Glenballoch

River Calder

Dalballoch

Finish
Newtonmore

Glen Banchor

Allt Madagain

B9150

A 9

A 86

gan

River Spey

A889

A 9

ABOVE: THE CREAG MEAGAIDH HILLS FROM GEAL CHARN

RIGHT: THE ROLLING TOPS OF THE MONADHLIATH FROM ABOVE THE UPPER
REACHES OF THE RIVER SPEY

•

the south, the Great Glen in the west and the A9 in the east, tapering out above Strathdearn in the north. If it contained just one superb mountain – a Lochnagar or a Buachaille Etive Mór – it would receive infinitely more walkers than come today, when many visit out of duty rather than love. Glen Banchor and Glen Markie make deep incisions into the Monadhliath on its southern side and are extremely attractive in their own right, but for many walkers the real problem with the area is the high ground itself. What is usually the principal attraction turns out to be the biggest drawback, and the ground over 2300 feet (700 m) or so is written off as featureless and boring. The four summits over 3000 feet (914 m) are all found in the south-eastern corner, their rounded tops separated by deep-cut glens, and a huge expanse of upland peat bog can make extremely tedious going at many times of the year. Yet even if comparatively few people have set foot on these hills, they have been seen by almost everyone who has explored the western Cairngorms, and their bulk is obvious to travellers going north on the A9. So why are the Monadhliath featured in this book of wilderness walks? They are included for two reasons: first and most important, the Monadhliath are transformed in winter, when they offer a relatively safe introduction to the world of winter walking and, better still, to the addictive challenge of ski touring. Secondly, they are best explored in a multi-day trip, where a number of alternatives are possible, some of which can be useful if bad weather rules out the very highest tops of the Cairngorms.

In truth, I decided to undertake my winter trip through the Monadhliath at short notice. After one of the mildest winters for many years, snow had now started to fall and for over a week considerable quantities had been deposited. On the lower land it tended to melt during each day but on the higher ground a good cover seemed to be building up, although I was uncertain as to what condition it might be in. I had been out for a number of day walks, but I had felt increasingly frustrated and wanted to escape from the office. The high Cairngorm tops were ruled out by the poor weather conditions, and I thought that the snow might well be unstable in many places. So I decided to explore the Monadhliath instead. Unlike the Cairngorms, where you can ask any number of people about the conditions, my journey was going to be a trip into the unknown, a thought that also appealed to me.

Going by oneself into such an environment is not something to be undertaken lightly, and everyone must judge his or her own competence for such a trip. In winter conditions carrying the appropriate equipment is vital, but that equipment is only of real use when accompanied by the knowledge of how best to use it. What might prove a minor inconvenience in summer can have disastrous consequences in winter. Yet the heightened awareness that comes from making an expedition at this time of year is an attraction in its own right, together with knowing that few people will be about in the hills. I had thought carefully about what gear to take and kept debating about whether taking my touring skis would be the best plan, but knowing neither the extent of the snow cover nor its condition I opted to save weight and left them behind. Instead I took an ice-axe and crampons, a good winter sleeping-bag, a reliable tent, an excellent stove, and the usual other bits and pieces. I always take a set of walking-poles and, as it turned out, these proved absolutely vital.

Garva Bridge to Loch Dubh

I was given a lift to Garva Bridge to the west of Laggan where the public road currently ends. The morning was idyllic, with the sun stroking the mountaintops and oystercatchers flying alongside the vehicle. For anyone travelling in the area on public transport, one option is possible: the post-bus from Newtonmore calls at Laggan on its way to Kinloch Laggan and can offer transport on all but Sundays and holidays (including a number of local ones). Other than the tediousness of walking on tarmac, the road west of Laggan is pleasant enough especially once the reservoir beyond the Spey Dam is reached.

Once the River Spey has been crossed at the head of the dam, the walking is on General Wade's road, which leads all the way through the Corrieyairack Pass to Fort Augustus. General Wade is credited with being both a soldier and a road-builder, although today he is most likely to be remembered for his civil engineering feats (which also included bridge construction) rather than his military prowess. It is claimed that he gave the Highlands of Scotland its first properly constructed roads. Wade was Irish by birth, and his early military service included periods in Flanders and Spain between 1692 and 1710. However, in 1724 he became Commander-in-Chief, North Britain, and during his posting he built well over 200 miles (320 km) of military roads in the Highlands, including the roads to Inverness from both Dunkeld and Fort Augustus. The Corrieyairack Pass is often thought of as one of his principal achievements, although he did not invent the route, which had previously been used by drovers.

In fact Garva Bridge itself is also one of Wade's constructions and has been little altered by the passing years. I had waited until arriving at the bridge, where I would start the walk, before I made my final plans, as I had considered a number of alternatives. I was determined to get away, and one possibility, had the weather looked unpromising, was to walk through the pass itself, either all the way to Fort Augustus or perhaps turning off into Glen Tarff and making my return over the remote ground further north of the Corrieyairack Pass. Other itineraries were also possible, but travelling in the mountains in winter has taught me one important lesson, which is not to make too many firm plans. In my view it is far better to have an overall strategy but to

The summit of Carn Dearg looking across Strath Spey to the
distant swell of the Cairngorms

•

keep it in the background and adapt it to the prevailing conditions by being prepared to be as flexible as possible and not getting tied to just one destination.

Today, though, I seemed, for the moment at least, to have struck lucky and intended to travel north-east, opting for either Kingussie or Newtonmore as potential destinations. This flexibility turned out to be a wise decision and allowed me to enjoy the hills to the full without worrying about arbitrarily imposed objectives. In summer, planning a multi-day trip is easy; barring the most unforeseen circumstances, it will turn out pretty much as expected. But in winter different rules apply. I always measure my rate of progress not in terms of miles covered but of the time I have been out, with always a thought that retreat can be the best option.

Shouldering my rucksack at the bridge and setting out alongside the Féith Talagain, I noticed immediately that this morning was far colder than the preceding ones, resulting in the snow being right down to the road. I was following a track on the eastern side of the stream; the track, at best, was indistinct at first, but higher up it was virtually lost under the soft new snow. My first peak was Beinn Sgiath, sometimes considered the southern summit of Geal Charn, itself the most westerly Munro in this group. I settled into a steady pace, watching the water running an icy stained-peat colour in the burn. Sometimes I need to spend some time in the hills to consider a particular problem away from the day-to-day pressures of the office, and this was true today. I had been thinking about how we rely on making assumptions – whether about a particular problem or about other people. In fact, I was thinking that such assumptions must dominate our lives.

As I began the long haul up the easy-angled slope to Beinn Sgiath, I began to think about this business of making assumptions in more detail. For over two years the argument had been raging about the proposed funicular railway planned for the Cairngorm ski development. Ostensibly, the plan was to replace some of the ageing chairlifts with the funicular, but the real issues were more fundamental than simply renewing outdated equipment. I had no desire to see the funicular built but had become increasingly depressed with the entrenched attitudes displayed by both sides in this long-running battle. Having supported the conservation movement for years, I was especially depressed by the way the various conservation bodies appeared to have conducted their campaign. Many attitudes still seemed rooted in the blunt protest politics of two decades ago, and in my opinion a more sophisticated approach was now necessary. Each side seemed to be making a number of assumptions about the other, assumptions that made any progress impossible as insults were hurled from each entrenched position. I was still thinking through the consequences of this when I was interrupted by a snow shower passing overhead and by the ground underfoot. My own trivial assumptions about the conditions were proving incorrect. I had expected the snow to get consolidated as I gained height, but this had not happened. In fact, the year had been exceptional in terms of weather. January and February were unseasonably warm, and the usual snow base had not formed. Indeed, by March nearly all the snow had melted, and the chairlift company had started to lay off some of its seasonal workers. Now, at the beginning of April, the temperature had suddenly dropped, and there was a belated return to winter conditions and a number of heavy snowfalls. But these had come too late to form a proper base, and the snow underfoot was soft, making for heavy going.

As I plodded towards the summit I would pick a line where the tops of the heather poked through the snow, hoping that I could keep out of the depressions and gullies. I would make reasonable progress for a few minutes and then unexpectedly sink right in – sometimes only a foot or so, but quite often I would fall into a gully and have to heave myself out with the poles. Uttering a few curses, I clung to the hope that conditions would be better once I reached the highest ground. Unless the conditions improved, my progress would be painstaking but there was some compensation in having picked the clearest day in the last week and more.

Reaching the summit of Beinn Sgiath took longer than I hoped, and a band of deep snow some 20 or 30 feet (6 or 9 m) high just below the summit caused me to ponder a while. Eventually, after a couple of false attempts that saw me sinking in up to my armpits, I managed to find a way through, zigzagging upwards in order to make progress. At first I wandered around the summit expecting to find an area scoured clean by the wind, but the constantly changing conditions of the last few days had meant that there was no prevailing wind and everywhere was now covered to a similar depth.

The summit was a good vantage point, especially down into Geal Charn's deep eastern corrie and across into deep Glen Markie. Looking back over my route, I could see the fine hills beyond Garva Bridge, Creag Meagaidh looking particularly striking with its top illuminated by a strong shaft of sunlight. As I made my way across to Geal Charn, losing 165 feet (50 m) or so only to gain another 300 feet (90 m), I looked right into the deep corner of the upper corrie that separates both hills and through the impressive 'window' that has been carved, over the centuries, by the ice, Uinneag Coire an Lochain (marked only on the 1:25 000 map). Again there were bands of soft snow to get through both between the summits and on the final approach to Geal Charn, but before long I was on my second top. Standing by the prominent cairn that was plastered with ice, I surveyed the landscape to the west and north looking out over a vast upland area of the Monadhliath. With the sun striking the fresh snow it presented a magnificent sight. In the foreground Loch na Lairige was the only prominent feature, with much of its surface covered by snow. I could see a large herd of deer and, in the far distance beyond, the beginning of the prominent glen containing the River Killin.

I now decided to follow the ridge north-eastwards, knowing that I needed to avoid losing height and dropping into Glen Markie itself. I hoped that the going would be

Overleaf: The cliff-girt waters of remote Loch Dubh

•

easier underfoot, assuming that the wind would have scoured the loose snow from the high ground. This was true to some extent, but any depression I came to was filled with blown snow and the ritual of sinking in and struggling out would start once again. I had soon realized that the likelihood of needing either ice-axe or crampons was remote; they stayed in the sack for the duration of this trip.

Half-way between Geal Charn and point 875 I stopped for a quick bite to eat, and starting off again resumed my thoughts about the current conservation debate and my questioning about our assumptions. Could we, I wondered, divorce the current conservation debate about wild places and their use from a more general holistic framework? In other words, should we be looking for a more widely based approach that set this debate in the broader context of how we treat the whole environment and how we assess our priorities? I know of people who vocally oppose all developments in some-where like the Cairngorms but then travel thousands of miles in their cars inflicting their own pollution on others. Of course, it is hard to accept that we might all need to curtail some aspects of our own personal freedom, but unless we begin to accept that such measures may be necessary they may ultimately have to be forced on us. Striking a balance is the difficulty, but we often travel as sole occupants of a car when other a lternatives are more socially acceptable. I am always surprised that people who never use a train are so certain about how poor it is! Of course, we are all blind to our own faults and again I was back to this business of making assumptions, especially about other people.

Taking turns to look east to the Cairngorm tops and west towards the deer forest of Corrieyairack and Glendoe, I made steady progress to point 875 (grid reference 578609) and continued onwards across this upland wilderness to Carn na Crìche. I thought how difficult it is to represent an area like this on a map. Only by looking at the 1:25 000 Ordnance Survey sheet did I get a real sense of the area and how it is dominated by the peat hags. The going was never particularly easy, but I was thoroughly enjoying myself, pleased to have escaped from my daily routine. I was delighted with how the weather was holding up and marvelled at the clear blue skies, the high cumulus cloud and the almost constant sunshine. I had not expected such a bonus and was try-ing not to be complacent, for a sudden change would alter everything. If a storm came in, good navigational skills, accurate mapreading and counting my paces would be vital. Nevertheless, my progress was not as quick as I would have liked, and I began to think about the remainder of my route in some detail. In better conditions it would have been possible to have kept to the tops, taking in Carn Odhar na Crìche, Carn Bàn, Meall a' Bhothain and Carn Sgùlain. However, I also wanted to explore more of this area with a view to searching out some good routes for future ski tours, and I wanted to know which places held the snow best. So I dropped off the plateau before Carn Odhar na Crìche and made my own way across the upper part of Allt Odhar, which was lost under feet of blown-in snow. Today, skiing would have been difficult, but I wondered how snowshoes would have performed. I had occasionally seen them in outdoor shops but did not know anyone who had used them regularly in Scotland. Now would have been a good opportunity to give them a real test.

I was delighted to find large accumulations of snow on the southern side of Carn Odhar na Crìche and contoured around the mountain, finally crossing the Red Burn at the very topmost finger of Glen Markie. By now it was after five o'clock, and I had seen no one all day; overhead I had noticed a couple of planes flying at altitude. One helicopter going south from its Inverness base had surprised me when it came over one of the tops but it soon passed. Looking at the shadow cast in the snow of myself, rucksack and poles, I could have easily been in Greenland. Mine were the only human tracks in the snow and I could see them providing clear evidence of my passing for a mile and more behind me. My only company during the day had been the animals and birds that inhabit the area and which are not used to much human intrusion. I had passed large herds of deer and virtually rubbed shoulders with a number of ptarmigan. I saw many mountain hares that had been fooled by the weather and whose coats had already turned from their winter white back to brown and which now stood out clearly against the snow. The few grouse I saw simply seemed disorientated and forlorn.

Similarly fooled by the weather, I had remembered to bring dark glasses but had stupidly forgotten to put in any sun lotion and for a couple of hours had felt my face starting to burn. The sun had also had its effect underfoot, the snow softening as the day progressed. Now I was often sinking in up to my waist and beyond, and extracting myself from such situations was tiring. I was relishing exploring this region but found that the snow cover was often not where I assumed it to be. I expected the gullies to be filled in but was surprised that some areas of relatively flat land also held large quantities of snow and reasoned that an area like this, full of peat hags, is not truly flat. Hence, snow fills in and is held in every little hollow, but seeing where these hollows are then becomes impossible. At one moment I would be walking from one tussock of heather to another; the next step would find me sinking straight in.

For the last hour or so I had been keeping an eye on the weather with the knowledge that the recent days had been unsettled and that today might be a rare bonus. I do not believe in a sixth sense as such, but looking around I felt there were the first signs emerging that today's superb conditions might not hold. My original thought had been to camp high up, but now I questioned the wisdom of this plan and adopted an alternative, deciding instead to use a bothy I knew of lower down. I crossed to the cliffs above the remote and lonely Loch Dubh and walked along them from above Coire nan Laogh to the prominent outcrop of Sròn nan Laogh (marked only on the 1:25 000 map). Looking down 655 feet (200 m) into the heart of the coire was magnificent but bleak. The black rocks protruding through the snow cover lent a sombre atmosphere to the whole scene and the ridge of Carn Dearg opposite looked similarly purposeful. I needed to descend to the Loch, and that became more difficult the lower I got. Finally, just a few yards from the bothy, I broke through the snow for a final time but not before

CARN DEARG FROM DALBALLOCH IN GLEN BANCHOR

•

my right foot had felt the icy water from a hidden stream ooze in and give me a rude awakening. I cursed the final few steps, but even my temporary discomfort could not blind me to the magnificence of the scene, with the rocks above the loch thrown into sharp relief by the snow and the frozen waterfall standing out in eerie silence.

Opening the bothy door took some effort, for the inside was partially filled with snow and it was clear that no one had stayed here for some time. I made good use of the solitary table and quickly had the stove roaring away; within a short time I'd had plenty to drink and eaten a barely passable instant meal. I got out my headtorch, looked at the map and then the reality of my day finally began to sink in. I had been out for slightly less than 12 hours and yet had covered fewer than that number of miles. I was pleased with my day but exhausted, with aching calf muscles testimony to my exertions. I normally make notes of the day, but that night I was too tired even to do that. I had a final brew, put my mat and sleeping-bag on the floor and crawled in. Bliss!

Some time after midnight I reluctantly got up for a call of nature and although half-asleep noticed that there was a good six inches (fifteen cm) of fresh snow outside the door. At first I thought it might have drifted, but a lack of wind made that theory somewhat unlikely. In any case, explanations could wait until the morning.

Loch Dubh to Newtonmore

I got up just after seven, awoken by the light streaming in through the one window. My boots and gaiters had frozen during the night, but I managed to get them on and soon had a cup of hot coffee in my hand. While the water was boiling I had gone outside and discovered that over nine inches (twenty-three cm) of snow had fallen and had transformed the whole corrie. The frozen waterfall could no longer be seen, and nearly all the rocks had been similarly covered. Spindrift was blowing off the ridge leading up to Carn Dearg and with more snow in the air the prospects did not look encouraging. Over breakfast I was brought back once again to thinking about assumptions. Originally, I had planned a two-day trip, but as things were turning out that was not going to be the best option. I had got the best from the day before by responding to the weather and by altering my plans accordingly, which had resulted in a very long but fulfilling day. Now I must likewise be prepared to be flexible.

Leaving the bothy, I was still undecided on my best course of action, but that soon became apparent. Within yards I was struggling, and with the new snow concealing even the merest helpful detail from the ground ahead, I was floundering around and sinking right in. Looking up, it was obvious that the weather was changing rapidly for the worse. The most sensible course of action was to make my way down Glen Banchor to Newtonmore. It was a decision I was loath to make but one that turned out to be correct.

I knew where the track from Loch Dubh went, but today there was no sign of it. I was sure I was either on or very near to it but, even so, my progress was miserly. It took me an hour and 40 minutes to reach the river crossing by Dalballoch Cottage, which was only two and a half miles (four km) down the glen. Today a number of sheep had sought refuge in this ruined building and stared out at me from the window and door. Only when I passed the deserted house of Glenballoch did the going significantly improve. Glen Banchor is one of the most attractive glens in this part of the world, and I found walking down it no hardship. I paused frequently to look back and remembered the names of many of the distinguished tops that mark the glen's perimeter. By the time I reached the outskirts of Newtonmore snow was falling constantly, and I thought how lucky I had been to snatch such a brief interlude at a time when most people had stayed indoors. I had not really sorted out my thoughts, and the questioning of various assumptions remained. What I had achieved was a superb day and a half in a landscape that, while not near to challenging Scotland's finest, has charms of its own – one assumption fewer to worry over.

CHAPTER EIGHT

THE ISLE OF SKYE, TROTTERNISH RIDGE

A HEAVENLY EXPEDITION

•

Richard Else

A fine two-day walk along Skye's other ridge

MAP: *OS 1:50 000 Sheet 23*
START: *Kilmaluag. Grid Ref: 433733.*
FINISH: *By A855 just north of Portree. Grid Ref: 488454*
LENGTH: *18 miles (29 km)*
APPROXIMATE TIME: *2 days*
TERRAIN: *Once the ridge has been reached, good walking on
short-cropped turf. Care is required in bad visibility*
ACCOMMODATION: *Many good hotels, guest-houses and b&bs in Portree. Also similar accommodation at Staffin
and Flodigarry. In the summer demand can be high and advance booking is essential*

In the way of islands we were in Gus's taxi but John was our driver. We'd not been in the vehicle for five minutes, and the crack (friendly conversation) had already begun. Helped by the traditional music coming from the car's cassette and hitting on a common interest, we were already deep into the merits of various accordions. John was proud of his vintage Hofner 'squeezebox' and recalled how he had struggled to buy it. At the time its cost had seemed a fortune, but it was now worth many times the original figure. The taxi was making its winding 23-mile (37-km) journey north from Portree to the tiny community of Kilmaluag at the northern tip of the island. As we passed the instantly recognizable outline of The Storr, I glanced into the windswept landscape as John recounted tales of his regular Saturday gigs in the bar of the Royal and how, as Sunday was the only day he didn't drive, he

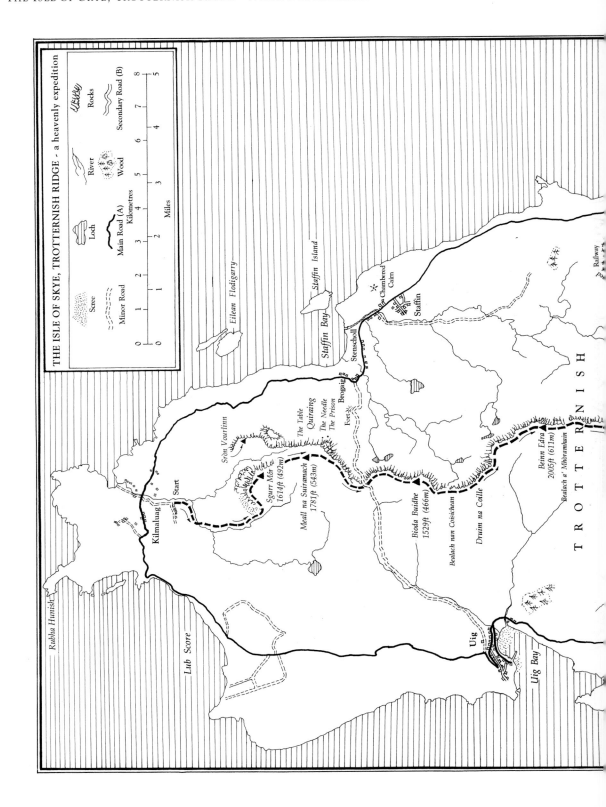

THE ISLE OF SKYE, TROTTERNISH RIDGE - a heavenly expedition

Scree
Minor Road
Loch
Main Road (A)
River
Wood
Rocks
Secondary Road (B)

Kilometres
Miles

Rubha Hunish

Lub Score

Eilean Flodigarry

Sròn Vourlinn

Sgurr Mòr
1614ft (492m)

Meall na Suiramach
1781ft (543m)

The Table
Quiraing
The Needle
The Prison

Kilmaluag

Start

Fort

Brogaig

Stenscholl

Staffin Bay

Staffin Island

Chambered
Cairn

Staffin

Bioda Buidhe
1529ft (466m)

Bealach nan Coisichean

Druim na Coille

Beinn Edra
2005ft (611m)

Bealach a' Mhoramhain

T R O T T E R N I S H

Uig

Uig Bay

Railway

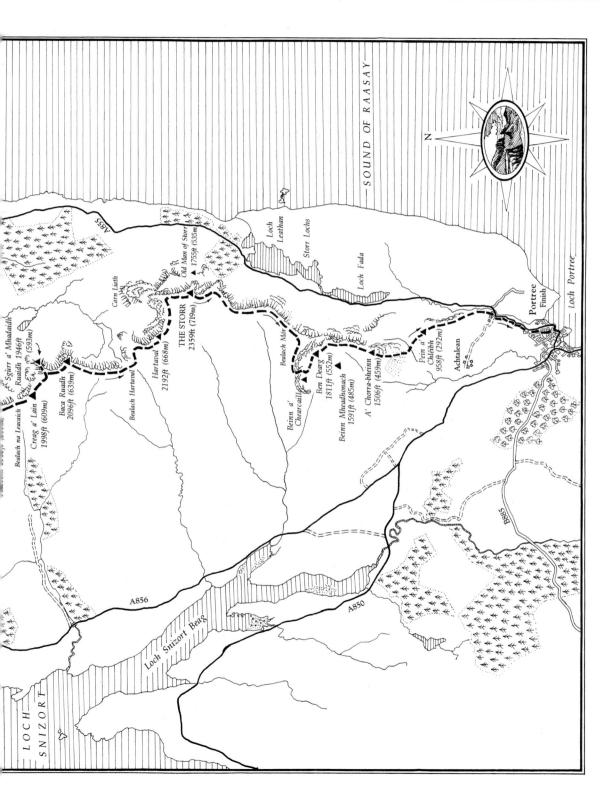

SOUND OF RAASAY

N

Loch Portree

Loch Leathan

Storr Lochs

Loch Fada

Old Man of Storr 1755ft (535m)

Carn Liath

Sgùrr a' Mhadaidh Ruadh 1946ft (593m)

Bealach na Leacaich

Creag a' Lain 1998ft (609m)

Baca Ruadh 2096ft (639m)

Bealach Hartaval

Hartaval 2192ft (668m)

THE STORR 2359ft (719m)

Bealach Mòr

Beinn a' Chearcaill

Ben Dearg 1811ft (552m)

Beinn Mheadhonach 1591ft (485m)

A' Chorra-bheinn 1506ft (459m)

Beinn a' Chlèibh 958ft (292m)

Achtalean

Portree
Finish

A855

A856

A850

B885

LOCH SNIZORT

Loch Snizort Beag

could indulge in a few wee drams (in his case gin because 'whisky doesn't agree with me whereas gin does no harm') and 'a long lie' in bed the next morning. By the time we passed Staffin he wished us good luck, with a reminder that 'two Germans had perished up there'. When he dropped us off at the sharp bend in the tiny road that heads south from Kilmaluag (grid reference: 433733) he suggested that, this being a Saturday, the bar of the Royal might be a better option than the elements of the exposed Trotternish Ridge. We heaved our rucksacks out of his boot and said our goodbyes with the band still playing on the car stereo but vanishing instantly on another strong gust of wind.

Kilmaluag to Beinn Edra
·

My mind was a jumble of thoughts as Meg and I put the rucksacks on our backs, instinctively zipped up our fleeces and set our faces right into the gale. Philosophically, I had always felt that a landscape and its people were inextricably interlinked, and a half-hour chat with John again reaffirmed that. For him the music, landscape, language, people and culture made one whole, or what I called the 'Skyeness' of it all. A week earlier I had met for the first time the Reverend Norman Drummond, who is the chairman of the BBC Board of Governors in Scotland and whose parish in Staffin we had just driven through. During our chat he had asked, with disarming frankness and an impish smile, what I felt about the spirituality of the mountains, adding, 'not just from a religious viewpoint'. We had met during a post-match wake after the Scotland v. England rugby international, which was hardly conducive to a long philosophical debate. What I failed to tell Norman (who has more than a passing interest in these fine hills) was that he had, with an unnerving accuracy, hit on an area of enquiry that had fascinated me for years.

I resolved to consider this question once more during the next two days, but now there was a more immediate problem – this wind! The Scottish Mountaineering Club's guide, *The Islands of Scotland*, has a phrase that suggests the longer you stay in Skye the more chance you have of getting better weather. This truism has probably comforted many visitors crouching in the entrances of dank tents or looking out through steamy windows, but for the last eight or ten weeks it simply would not have been true, as one rainy front followed another through the whole of the West Coast. For what seemed like for ever I had been watching successive days' weather forecasts with black rain clouds covering the west, fuming inwardly and recalling those words from the SMC guide, rhetorically asking: 'How long is long?'

Now, with a possible two-day break in the early March weather, we had made a dash for Skye hoping we could escape into the hills. Meg had more sense than to ask how I felt, but my face probably spoke volumes: 'optimistically pessimistic' was my verdict. I had wanted to walk the complete Trotternish Ridge in one outing and did not want anything to spoil it. In spite of exploring well beyond Skye's magnet of the Black Cuillin, I had never left enough time on the many previous trips to do the whole of the ridge, and walking it had assumed an importance well beyond its mere height and length. Indeed, for the most part this walk is on delightfully easy ground; route-finding is never a real problem and the total distance (assuming you take Sgurr Mór in the north as your first summit and the diminutive Pein a' Chléibh at the southern end as the last top) is no more that 18 miles (29 km); and the highest individual mountain is the Storr at 2359 feet (719 m). You could even do the whole lot in one marathon day! You could, but in my view you would miss many of the features that make this not merely a fine walk but a real expedition far beyond any bare statistics. An added bonus is that few people make this journey through a landscape that is steeped in history. As one mile gives way to another, one summit to the next, it is clear that the ridge is a real challenge, although the reasons for this only become clear as you make the journey south. Put quite simply, the Trotternish Ridge is one of the finest walks in Britain. If walks were awarded stars or rosettes like hotels or music recordings this would get all five.

In many ways the first mile or two across the rough ground south of Kilmaluag and the 1150-odd feet (350-odd m) of ascent onto the summit of Sgurr Mór is as hard as the walking gets. Adopting a 'full steam ahead' approach is far too easy, racing up conscious only of the miles that lie ahead, but that would mean neglecting much of interest in the area. Indeed, if we had not been pressed for time I would have started at Rubha Hunish, which is the most northerly point on the whole island and can make an indisputably fine starting-point to the whole enterprise.

In spite of being continually buffeted by the wind (which had reduced our conversation to prolonged periods of silence punctuated by the occasional short, shouted phrase) we had made good time to the top of Sgurr Mór, with the final pull up to the summit far less steep than most of the ascent. Just over an hour and 45 minutes after leaving John's taxi, we stood on our first top. Suddenly we were on the ridge itself and our adventure had begun! We had stayed in Portree overnight and with the days ever lengthening had indulged in a hearty breakfast before the taxi-ride north. As a result it was now already mid-morning, yet we still spent a few minutes on the summit and took stock of the scene laid out before us. To the east the mainland hills of Torridon and Applecross form a background to a landscape that, nearer to hand, is dominated by the Islands of Rona and Raasay (the latter of which has two smaller islands, Eilean Tigh and Eilean Fladday, nestling around its shore). To the north of Rubha Hunish are a smaller cluster of islands, including Fladda-chùain and Lord Macdonald's Table, and a short distance east the solitary landmass of Eilean Trodday.

One of the jewels of Trotternish: the Storr in winter splendour

•

This northern part of the island is steeped in history, as anyone who has read Seton Gordon's excellent *Highways and Byways in the West Highlands* will know. This book, by one of Scotland's great natural historians, was written in the early 1930s and is as fascinating today as when it was first published. Gordon not only had a naturalist's eye but also an historian's inquisitiveness, and he has a wealth of detail about the history of this area. To the north-east is Sròn Vourlinn, described by Seton Gordon as a 'grim and dark' peak, locally called Sron Bhiornal, which has its own legend that reflects the mixed heritage of Skye. According to tradition, during the Norse occupation of the island a princess named Biornal wanted to be buried on the mountain so that she might be in sight of Norway. While there is nothing to mark her grave, the tradition maintains that she is buried on a grassy ledge about 70 feet (21 m) below the summit and her resting-place is the first soil of Skye to feel the north wind from Norway. Gordon, with a characteristic Scottish pragmatism, speculates that getting her body to such a position would have been difficult because the ground below the ledge falls away in a sheer precipice and concludes that she must have been lowered down by ropes, while everyone else would have been forced to climb down in order to bury her. This must have been an arduous enterprise. Perhaps after such an undertaking no one had the energy to build a cairn marking the spot.

The next mile is a gentle descent and rise that took us to the top of Meall na Suiramach and a height gain of 165 feet (50 m). Although this is the highest section on this first part of the ridge (which ends at the Uig to Staffin road) and looks somewhat round and uninteresting when seen from the west or north, its importance lies in its location. Its grassy top is marked by one of three Ordnance Survey triangulation pillars passed on the walk south and apart from the column being constructed of stones and cement rather than the usual concrete there is little else to distinguish this peak. Yet walk a few yards east to the clifftops that are a constant feature of this route and the view is spectacular as you look down on the complex form of the Quiraing.

Peter Drummond's *Scottish Hill and Mountain Names* is an indispensable work. He suggests that Quiraing means 'pillared enclosure' from the Gaelic words 'cuith raing' with the 'pillar' almost certainly referring to the prominent feature of The Needle. According to another placename writer, Alexander Forbes, quoted by Drummond, the Gaelic words themselves come originally from the two Norse words '*kvi-rand*' and '*quoy-rand*'. Such linguistic intricacy gives a fascinating insight into the long, mixed history of Skye. Indeed, the history of this part of the island is, I think, one of the most fascinating in the whole of Scotland. Yet its geography and geology are no less interesting. Both Meg and I normally are far more interested in the human rather than physical dimension of a landscape, but here the latter is in sharp and dramatic focus. At the risk of offending those with specialist knowledge, it is a series of massive, spectacular landslips on the eastern side of Trotternish that have brought this superb ridge into being. So while the land slopes gently away to the west, there is always a steep drop to the east guarded by a succession of cliffs that can be easily breached only in a few places. (Hence, in the event of really bad weather, an escape to the west will often be the preferable option.) These land movements have resulted in such dramatic forms as the Quiraing, which is made up of a number of distinct features. This jumble of volcanic rock contains a large, flat area not surprisingly called The Table, the reason for its name immediately obvious when it is seen from above but hidden from view when approached from below, a tall slender finger of rock known as The Needle which is especially prominent when approaching from the south, and a natural stronghold, The Prison (occasionally called The Castle by some writers), just to the south-east. The whole is a jumbled mass of rock structures, and little wonder that it is said cattle were hidden in this labyrinthine collection of rocky towers during hostile raids when local knowledge and cunning might well have been more important than brute strength.

Such a landscape always repays further study, and two pamphlets from the Skye Environmental Centre (see Further Reading at the end of the book) provide a good introduction. Leaving Quiraing my thoughts returned to the history of this landscape and, with the continual gale making it almost impossible to talk to Meg, I became lost in my own thoughts and began pondering Norman Drummond's question about the spirituality of the landscape and especially the mountains. On reading the pamphlets I discovered that Scotland's oldest inhabitants were found on the neighbouring island of Rùm: Mesolithic hunter-gatherers dating back to, perhaps, 6000 years BC. In the north of Skye itself is evidence of chambered cairns, hillforts, duns and brochs. ('Duns' were fortified dwellings while 'brochs' were massive archaeological achievements, measuring up to 65 feet (20 m) in diameter, serving as fortified homesteads; brochs were the peak of dry-stone architecture.) Taken as a whole, these buildings provide evidence that this landscape was peopled from around 4500 BC onwards. Moreover, we are still expanding our knowledge about our forefathers as I found from a newspaper report that week which told of an Iron Age cave that had just been discovered, with many implements intact, on the eastern side of the island, making a treasure-trove for historians to investigate.

Making our way south-west from Quiraing we stopped before the Uig–Staffin road for a quick bite to eat. As we sat in the heather looking eastwards to the tiny ribbon settlements of Brogaig, Stenscholl and Staffin, with their characteristic white dwellings, one aspect of the mountains' spirituality became clear. Here are settlements and communities in the real sense of both words, where the relationship with the environment must be one of cooperation rather than domination. I was moved to realize that an unbroken line links us back around 6000 years and that this landscape provided, to successive generations, not simply food and shelter but also an inspiration for a whole range of cultural and artistic achievements, including the beautiful pottery of the 'Beaker People' who came to Skye in around 2000 BC.

ABOVE: LOOKING SOUTH FROM THE QUIRAING

RIGHT: THE NEEDLE, GUARDING THE ENTRANCE TO THE CURIOUS
LANDSLIP OF THE QUIRAING

•

I continued thinking along these lines after we crossed the road and started the steady, rhythmical plod up to Bioda Buidhe (1529 feet/466 m). It has always amazed me that people whose existence must have been so hard and life expectancy so short in comparison with our own should have had time to build monuments like stone circles that, having no strictly useful purpose, provided a spiritual dimension to their lives. Similarly, I have always enjoyed walking at the extremities of the year, rather than in summer, to relish a more elemental relationship with the landscape.

We had met no one on our walk but had always been conscious of the force and the sheer stark beauty of nature as we toiled our way south. I had just started to think about how such journeys (when every mile of progress must be earned) bring a heightened sense of awareness when nature, with a timing worthy of the best actor, illustrated this perfectly. 'Look!' I called to Meg. Circling below us was a golden eagle. For a few minutes we watched its majestic form riding the air currents, first swooping one way and then another as it searched for prey, before it was obscured behind an intervening peak. It provided another highlight to a day that had been filled with many moments of pure joy. In such conditions as these, the spirituality of the mountains was all around us, and I thought it little wonder that settings such as these had inspired our finest writers, artists and composers for successive generations.

The descent from the summit of Bioda Buidhe is steepish but trouble free, losing some 460 feet (140 m) passing Bealach nan Coisichean to the flat, rough area known as Druim na Coille. The continual buffeting of the south-westerly wind had meant that Meg and I were not making quite the progress we had hoped for but, with the evenings lengthening, we had thought an extra hour's walking or so before putting up the tent might mean we could meet our target. Nature, however, had a different idea.

We started the long steady pull up to Beinn Edra, observing as we did so that the uphill sections never felt as steep as they looked, even when, as here, nearly 985 feet (300 m) of ascent was necessary. In spite of being able to see settlements to both the east and the west from almost everywhere on the route, we felt a sense of isolation walking by ourselves along the tops. Soon, there was no mistaking that what we had thought might be just a passing shower heralded a real deterioration in the weather. The rain, driven mercilessly by the gale, started in earnest as we made our way upwards. The mist came down; gloves were pulled out of the packs and hoods went up, meaning that we continued in silence but to the unremitting machine-gun-like sound of the rain hitting our hoods. In spite of the unseasonal mildness, by the time we arrived at the summit (and the second triangulation pillar on the route) we were getting sodden and cold, with extremities chilled by the wind.

After a brief snatched conversation conducted by a series of shouts, we decided to press on, hoping for some improvement in the weather. A quick descent and reascent followed via Bealach a' Mhòramhain to Beinn Mheadhonach (marked simply as point 579 on the 1:50 000 map), but the weather was still appalling. In spite of not reaching our day's objective, we both simultaneously decided it was time to find as sheltered a spot as was possible in which to pitch the tent. My decision was motivated not so much by the cold and wet or the difficulty in simply standing upright but by a magic spell woven on me by the ridge itself. Earlier, I had enjoyed not just the view ahead but also the ever-changing landscape behind and the vistas to the west. This was a walk to be relished, and I would rather take more time the following day if it meant a chance to enjoy it to the full. We dropped down westwards but thought, with the wind coming from this direction, we would be lucky to find any real shelter. Mentally, we were preparing to put up our tent in the teeth of the storm. We were very surprised, therefore, that, having dropped down less than 330 feet (100 m), we found ourselves sheltered from the worst of the wind. By now we were both totally sodden, yet, putting up the tent, we knew we would shortly be able to have a brew going. Pure bliss! It was around five o'clock and we had been battling against the wind for over seven hours. No wonder we felt we had earned that first cuppa!

Beinn Edra to Portree

We had decided to get up before dawn the next morning and be on the move by first light, but it was Meg who made sure I heard the alarm. I hardly dared look out of the tent, but when I did so the sight was promising – a view confirmed by the barometer on my watch, which was showing a consistent rise in pressure. The mist was lingering on the tops, but the air was without a trace of yesterday's wind. As we set off I recalled Seton Gordon, who had noted the importance of the various old hill passes that connected east with west: at one time crossing the ridge was through necessity. I also wondered who had been the first to walk this challenging ridge in one continuous undertaking from north to south, speculating on the reason for their traverse. Was it the sighting of a fine aesthetic line running right down the spine of the island or for a more prosaic reason? I had assumed that Sheriff Alexander Nicholson, a pioneer of the Black Cuillin, might have been the original walker on this route, but looking at the first edition of the Scottish Mountaineering Club's guide to Skye found that Sheriff Penney had written about his traverse in March 1901. He noted:

> Sheriff Nicholson is alleged to have said that 'to ascend Storr and follow the mountain ridge the whole way till you come to the highroad near the Quiraing is no doubt one of the grandest promenades on Skye'… I have determined to follow his advice, although I have now as little doubt that he never did the tramp himself as I have that Scott 'never went by light of moon what could be seen at noon'!

I had also noted that Penney's outing had been from Portree northwards, whereas most of today's walkers take the opposite direction. On reflection, Meg and I both thought journeying north to south is the preferable option.

We had made good time ascending Groba nan Each (2057 feet/627 m), with the ridge narrowing slightly on the approach. Now we adopted a steady pace, savouring every bealach as much as the summits and pleased that our sodden clothes from the previous day were starting to dry in the early-morning breeze. To the east we could see the large patch of forestry adjoining the main road and, nearer at hand, the disused railway and road that lead to the former mine near Loch Cuithir. These tracks, together with dozens of lochans and other ribbons of water, were now all glistening in the sun, reminding me of the advantages of spending nights in high places. Looking eastwards, it is possible to bring the brain to life by trying to name the mountains etched on the skyline and running in both directions from the Applecross peninsula. There were equally superb views westwards across to Waternish and beyond.

After the preceding day's gale, the stillness of this morning was all the more pronounced. We followed a tiny path that in many places was indistinct and summits like Flasvein (1965 feet/599 m), Creag a' Lain (1998 feet/609 m), Sgùrr a' Mhadaidh Ruaidh (1946 feet/593 m) and Baca Ruadh (2096 feet/639 m) were passed as we kept marvelling at the panoramic views that were laid before us in all directions. As we made our way southwards, it was clear to both of us this particular morning that the real attraction in the route and what makes it a true wilderness outing is the undertaking of it as one expedition. There is the knowledge that once embarked on, the route needs a real commitment to see it through. In any event this southern section has a magnetic pull: it is not just that every mile walked is a mile less (in fact, such is the beauty of this section that many would be content for it to carry on for a few extra miles!) but that this is the most interesting section of the ridge and one that contains the highest summit – The Storr. From Baca Ruadh we were pleased to see that the mist, which had kept the very highest tops hidden for the last 24 hours, had now lifted and The Storr itself was in full view. Onwards!

With spirits high we crossed the plateau south of Baca Ruadh then lost about 500 feet (140 m) in our rocky descent to Bealach Hartaval. It was easy to get trapped into a 'let's just keep walking' mentality by this time, but we stopped long enough for a snack and took some photographs in the translucent light of the ridge. Out eastwards we noted the continually changing forms of Rona and Raasay, while to the west the light was less good, suggesting that the early part of the day might have been the best.

The traverse of Hartaval is a good prelude to The Storr itself and the corrie separating the summit of the former from Carn Liath is impressive. Meg had thought the 650-foot (200-m) trudge up to The Storr's summit might prove wearing, but the contours are evenly spaced and before long we were at 2359 feet (719 m) catching our breath by the Ordnance Survey column that marks the top. Like nearly everywhere

THE OLD MAN OF STORR, AS ANCIENT AS TIME ITSELF

•

along this ridge, looking eastwards gives a fabulous panoramic vista, but from here the view to the Old Man of Storr is not as spectacular as from the road. What is impressive, having walked the few feet to the cliff edge, is the space beneath your feet as the rock plunges about 650 feet (200 m) in a sheer vertical face. In bad weather or when the ground is slippery, some caution should be exercised here, for a bad slip would be lethal, although for many walkers a rush of vertigo will probably curtail any further investigation! It is hard not to judge this peak the highlight of the walk, particularly when, in clear weather, the views include the magnificent sight of the Black and Red Cuillin breaking the southern skyline.

Leaving The Storr, we had wondered if the rest of the walk might be something of a disappointment and a dreary return to everyday life. True, the best of the walk had now been completed, but the long steady descent from The Storr gave good views of both the route ahead, with the cliffs continuing to guard the eastern flank, and of the lonely sheet of water comprising Loch Leathan, Storr Lochs and Loch Fada. Ahead, Ben Dearg is the only summit on the route that cannot easily be directly ascended. Instead, it is best approached by a short detour west and then up a scree slope roughly half-way beween its summit and that of neighbouring Beinn a' Chearcaill. Incidentally, that does not take nearly as long as it might appear when seen looking up from Bealach Mór! South of here the land changes and areas of peat hags must be crossed, although they impede progress less than might be expected. There is a choice of routes here, but we kept just east of south via A' Chorra-bheinn and Pein a' Chléibh, losing height all the time. Now Portree beckoned and there was no doubting that the Trotternish Ridge was over. The road is finally reached just north of the town where the minor road to Achtalean forks west.

We both felt a sense of real excitement at having finished, a feeling usually associated with longer walks, and while the ridge is harder than the mileage suggests it is certainly no marathon but within the reach of any walker. It was clear that the few people out for a stroll this Sunday afternoon were bemused by our packs and walking-poles but, in spite of a few enquiring looks, we did not enlighten anyone about our adventure. We arrived back at the Cuillin Hills Hotel, threw the gear into the back of the Land Rover and headed straight inside. Time for not just a celebration but also for something deeper – to think once again about a precious time in a landscape that spoke volumes about the spirituality of the mountains which can only be inadequately described in words.

CHAPTER NINE

THE BEN-DAMPH AND COULIN FORESTS

ALONE AMONG FINE MOUNTAINS

•

Richard Else

An exploration of hills between Strathcarron and Torridon

Map: *OS 1:50 000 Sheet 25*
Start and finish: *Achnashellach railway station. Grid Ref: 003485. Alternatively,*
Coulags on the A896. Grid Ref: 964452
Length: *Approximately 20–24 miles (30–39 km), depending on the exact route taken*
Approximate time: *2 days*
Terrain: *A delightful exploration of this compact group of mountains*
Accommodation: *A choice of accommodation at Lochcarron and a hotel adjacent to the railway*
station at Strathcarron

A certain F. Reid Corson, writing in the early 1930s, began his book *Beyond the Great Glen – A Wayfaring Guide to the North-West Highlands* by stating that 'it is the considered opinion of qualified judges that the finest scenery in Britain lies north and west of the Great Glen of Scotland'. Today, almost all walkers will be more familiar with the man who wrote the foreword to the book, A. E. Robertson, the first Munroist, than with Corson himself, but this delightful book contains many valuable insights into the superb and varied landscape that is to be found beyond the Caledonian Canal. It is, Corson reminds us, a region that contains 'the great sea-lochs of the west, the hundred peaks of Ross-shire, the three unrivalled Inverness-shire glens, the Coolins of Skye and the strange isolated mountains of Sutherland'. Although much has changed in the 60-odd years since Corson penned those words (including an acceptance that 'Cuillin'

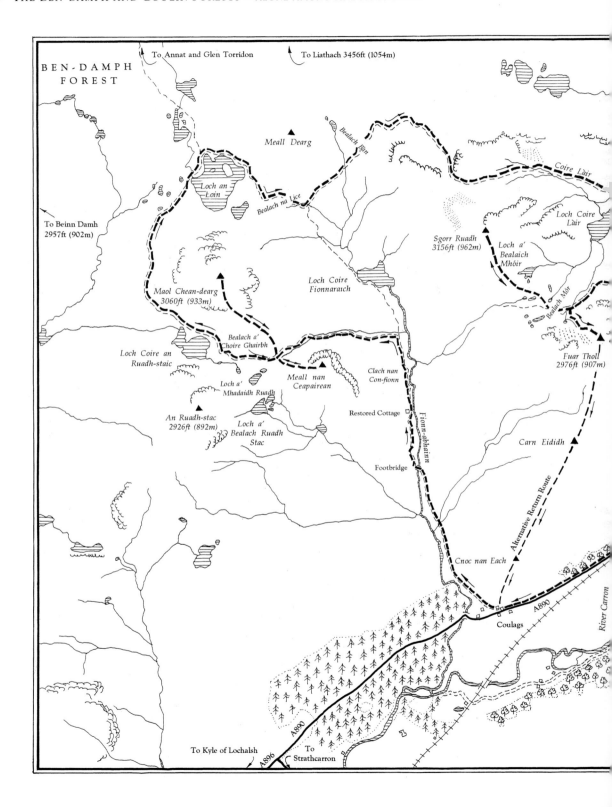

BEN-DAMPH
FOREST

To Annat and Glen Torridon

To Liathach 3456ft (1054m)

Meall Dearg

Bealach Ban

Coire Làir

Loch an
Loin

Bealach na Lice

To Beinn Damh
2957ft (902m)

Sgorr Ruadh
3156ft (962m)

Loch Coire
Làir

Loch a'
Bealaich
Mhóir

Bealach Mòr

Loch Coire
Fionnaraich

Maol Chean-dearg
3060ft (933m)

Bealach a'
Choire Ghairbh

Fuar Tholl
2976ft (907m)

Loch Coire an
Ruadh-staic

Meall nan
Ceapairean

Clach nan
Con-fionn

Loch a'
Mhadaidh Ruadh

Restored Cottage

Fionn-abhainn

Carn Eididh

An Ruadh-stac
2926ft (892m)

Loch a'
Bealach Ruadh
Stac

Footbridge

Alternative Return Route

Cnoc nan Each

Coulags

A800

River Carron

A800

To Kyle of Lochalsh

A896

To
Strathcarron

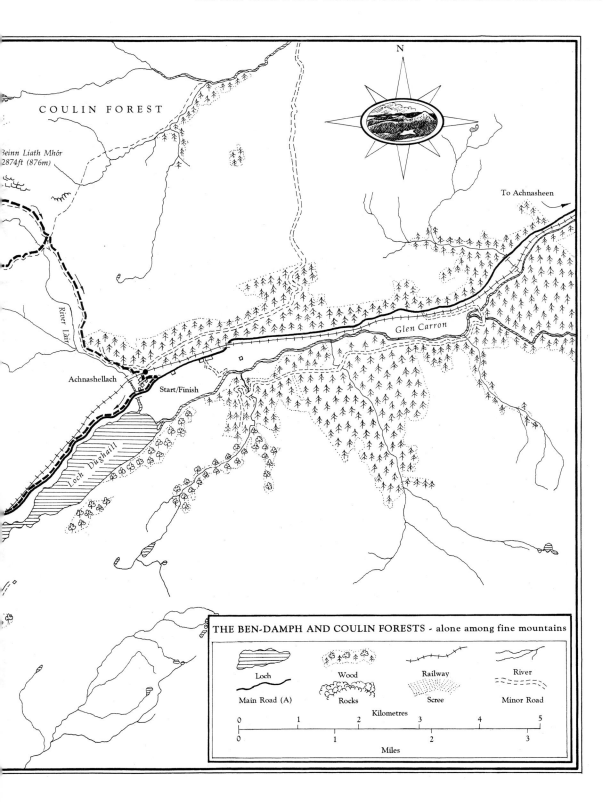

N

COULIN FOREST

Beinn Liath Mhór
2874ft (876m)

To Achnasheen

River Lair

Glen Carron

Achnashellach

Start/Finish

Loch Dughaill

THE BEN-DAMPH AND COULIN FORESTS - alone among fine mountains

Loch

Wood

Railway

River

Main Road (A)

Rocks

Scree

Minor Road

Kilometres

0   1   2   3   4   5

0   1   2   3

Miles

is the correct spelling), his assertion that relatively few hikers and campers know this magical area is still largely true.

For many years I had been exploring this region little by little, often linking routes together to make longer excursions and, on occasions, returning to savour favourite mountains more fully. Yet the area is so vast that there always remain places that I meant to explore more fully but somehow never quite found the time for. The hills that make up the Ben-damph and Coulin Deer Forests, sandwiched between Glen Torridon and Glen Carron, form one such group. In many ways they remain over-shadowed by such giants as Liathach and Beinn Eighe tantalizingly situated just to the north.

Travelling west of the Great Glen fills me with excitement and trepidation, excitement aroused by the shapely mountains, remote glens and spectacular sea lochs, trepidation caused by never being quite sure of what the weather holds in store. This is also a landscape that, for me at least, is characterized by a remoteness found nowhere else in Britain on such a scale. West of Garve both road and railway contour along Srath Bran to Achnasheen before turning south-west into Glen Carron. This country is typified by small, lonely, walled cemeteries tucked into the corners of fields, by solitary fishing-lodges and by the single-track railway itself, which forms such a vital link between the Kyle of Lochalsh and Inverness; low-flying jets, with the noise of their engines, are another characteristic feature.

The building of the railway is very much a story of hope and determination triumphing over adversity and is well documented in John Thomas's book *The Skye Railway*. The railway still allows good access to this area today, and I particularly like the idea of asking the conductor to make a stop at Achnashellach. Travelling on a Sprinter train is a cosy affair but it does force me to make decisions about equipment before leaving home. Given I hate making final choices at any time, this is a rigorous discipline because once I am on the train it is no use realizing that a vital item has been forgotten! Even today, getting out onto the single platform that was once a private station is an eerie experience as the train pulls away and I am left with just a rucksack and my own thoughts, thoughts that turned to Donald McLeod, the original stationmaster. His important title concealed a less-than-grand existence: for over 20 years he worked entirely by himself, completing a 14-hour day in summer and a 12-hour one in winter. His nearest colleague was five and a half miles (nine km) away at Strathcarron and the next one was eleven miles (eighteen km) east at Achnasheen. John Thomas paints a vivid picture of his weekly routine:

> *Manning his lonely outpost, he operated the signals and points, worked the telegraph, assisted with the shunting and cleaned the office as well as selling the occasional ticket and dealing with the meagre paperwork that his situation demanded.*

The railway between Dingwall and Strome Ferry opened in August 1870 but nearly another 30 years were to pass before it was extended to the current terminus at the Kyle of Lochalsh. In spite of being run in a somewhat unorthodox manner and suffering a catalogue of mishaps, including a station fire, storm damage and an accident at Achnashellach itself when a train literally ran away, there is no doubt that communications in this remote part of western Scotland were altered irrevocably by the arrival of the railway.

I left the station thinking about McLeod and his lonely life but soon my thoughts moved from the railway to the hills. Munro-baggers will be attracted to the mountainous area north of the railway by the trio of rocky isolated peaks – Beinn Liath Mhór, Maol Chean-dearg and, at 3156 feet (962 m), the highest of this group, Sgorr Ruadh. However, there are many more reasons to explore this fascinating wild area, and my particular route this early spring took in two of the Munros, the same number of lesser peaks (lesser in terms only of height, it should be added) together with what in America would be called superb back-country. However, many fine walks can be done around here, including a horseshoe around Coire Làir, so many variations are possible.

Coulags to Maol Chean-dearg

·

While the area boasts a number of stalkers' paths that have been well maintained in recent years and there are also rights of way to both Torridon and through the Coulin Forest, they do not diminish either the special character of the area or the sense that in any time other than high summer you are travelling through a genuine wilderness.

My plan involved a walk along the road for five miles (eight km) west before leaving it at Coulags (approximately two and a quarter miles/three and a half km east of the junction with the A890 Strathcarron road), where a sign indicates a right of way to Torridon and a good, well-defined path passes a modern white bungalow and, cutting through heather, follows the course of the Fionn-abhainn northwards upstream. I had travelled here through intermittent showers and wondered what the next few days would bring. The weather looked as if it could go either way and although my surroundings appeared uniformly grey, helped by almost 100 per cent cloud cover, the reality was quite different. As I wandered up to the wooden footbridge that crosses the burn just over a mile from the road, I realized I was suffering from a form of culture shock. I had just returned from nearly three weeks in the high Atlas of Morocco (see the postscript to this book), where the days had been exceptionally warm, the weather stable and the skies a Kodachrome blue. Now I was back in Scotland and having to

Above: Maol Chean-dearg and the distant Isle of Skye from Sgorr Ruadh

Right: The footpath beside the Fionn-abhainn

•

refocus my eyes to cope with a more restricted range of colours. Yet the effort was more than amply rewarded, for although the landscape at first appeared purely grey, in reality it was composed of shades of blue, brown and muted green. Another difference was that in Morocco we had, somewhat lazily, trekked with mules; now I was once again doing my own load-carrying in the steady pace of a long walk. Morocco had also been a social affair, with seven of us travelling together; now I was on my own. I was, for the moment at least, pleased to have just my own company and to be making decisions that affected only myself.

The footbridge over the Fionn-abhainn is built high, illustrating just how dangerous the burn can be in spate. Once on the western bank, you almost immediately pass the restored cottage that serves as a bothy outside the stalking season. So many writers have mentioned this isolated building that it is well known, which I think is a pity. Better, in my view, that people discover such places by chance or that their locations are spread by word of mouth. Too many of these shelters are being used by organized groups or as substitutes for paid accommodation rather than for their original purpose of providing rudimentary places to sleep in for travellers and hill-folk. I passed quickly on this occasion, noting just a solitary face at a window, and, looking up to a deteriorating sky, wondered if staying indoors might conceivably be the wiser option. From the bothy you can see Clach nan Con-fionn, a peculiar finger-shaped piece of rock higher up the glen where, according to legend, the giant Fionn is said to have tied his staghounds while hunting. On an earlier visit it had intrigued me that this legend should have been associated with such an isolated spot, and I had begun to think about the origin of the myths, legends and folklore that are so prevalent in the Highlands. Later, at home, I had sought to define these three aspects of country life when my partner, Meg, had with her usual historian's precision made a more relevant comment. 'If he were such a good houndsman he wouldn't have needed to have tied the dogs up while he went hunting,' she said, shattering in an instant this particular legend.

Today, any such musings were short-lived, for after I'd come to a fork in the track and taken the left-hand path, rain began to fall in the way that tells you immediately that the dry part of the day is now over for good. Although it begins in a quiet, almost reticent way, the message is unmistakable – this is not going to stop. I looked up to the Bealach a' Choire Ghairbh (unnamed on the 1:50 000 map), where I was heading for, between Meall nan Ceapairean and Maol Chean-dearg, and saw that the cloud base, which had never been high on that particular morning, was now down to around 1500 feet (450 m). The track that would lead me steadily upwards in a series of wide zigzags to the bealach was now a route into the mist and rain. During this first hour and more of the walk, I had already been relieved to experience a sense of letting go. As I concentrated on keeping the rain out and methodically gained height, I thought about friends who found it impossible to be parted from their mobile phones, e-mail or their centrally heated houses. My wallet getting wet in the top of the rucksack added to my thoughts – here money and credit cards have no value, but reliable equipment is everything. At around one o'clock I came to the top of the bealach at around 1805 feet (550 m) but I could see little and decided on a radical change of plan. Originally, I had thought I would climb at least two, possibly three of the surrounding tops before looking for a suitable campsite. Now, with the weather undoubtedly closing in, I made my way across the wet ground to the small lochan adjacent to Loch a' Mhadaidh Ruadh (again unnamed on the 1:50 000 map) and started to pitch my tent. This is normally a wonderful campsite with superb views in almost every direction but now the outlook consisted of swirling mist and beating rain. My thinking was that it would be best to have somewhere to come back to at the end of the day when I would be both sodden and, most probably, tired. The tent, now pitched, also allowed me the luxury of a hot brew and a quick snack before setting out to explore the surrounding mountains unencumbered by my pack and taking just a map, compass and walking-poles.

Being an eternal optimist – at least as far as walking in the west is concerned – I started to saunter up Meall nan Ceapairean in the mist. The rise is a gentle one of around 330 feet (100 m) or so, and very soon I was standing on the summit. I saw nothing from the top, but somewhat surprised myself by being unconcerned about this. Today there were no fine views to the eastern mountains, so pausing a while I stared into the whiteness and found myself thinking about two contrasting ascents I made a couple of years earlier on A' Mhaighdean in Letterewe. I had ascended this fine hill (usually described as the most isolated mainland Munro) one May and been rewarded with the most magnificent sunsets and breathtaking views down Fionn Loch and away westwards. A few weeks later I was again on its summit, but this time there was no view. My companion on this second occasion was John MacKenzie, Earl of Cromartie, and he said something that has stuck with me. Looking straight into the impenetrable gloom, he smiled and said, 'Hills in mist are actually much more interesting in some ways because you actually look at the small things: lichen on rock, crystals, all sorts of things.' Today in a similar situation I knew exactly what he meant but wondered how it could ever be explained to those who do not walk. On the face of it, getting enjoyment from spending days walking in the rain sounds pretty improbable.

As I descended with a general feeling of wellbeing, the mist lifted for a few moments to allow fine views of the lochs to the south of An Ruadh-stac, especially Loch a' Bealach Ruadh Stac (once more unnamed on the 1:50 000 map) and its adjacent lochans; the briefest of glimpses of Maol Chean-dearg (which dominates this small group) and the eastern face of An Ruadh-stac itself, which, sodden by the rain, had taken on a liquid appearance. Wild, beautiful country, was my immediate thought as I headed down, realizing that what I had always enjoyed was this stravaiging across wild land and wondering where my wanderings would take me next.

Peaks of the Coulin deer forest: Maol Chean-dearg and
An Ruadh-stac from Beinn Damh

•

In spite of the brief break in the weather, I knew things were getting worse rather than better and with water appearing to ooze out of every single crack I decided to leave An Ruadh-stac for another day and make for Maol Chean-dearg itself. Starting up the series of zigzags that lead from the bealach, I was once again lost in my own thoughts, which, not unnaturally, turned to my love of the outdoors. I remembered school days spent looking out of windows to distant bumps that were hardly hills but being fascinated by them none the less. Later I studied the writings of the romantic poets and the work of landscape photographers. Like many kids of the time, I discovered the outdoors at first hand through being part of a youth group and going off camping. I must have been 12 when I first went away and remember going into town with my parents to buy a sleeping-bag from the outdoor shop. I wonder if my mother, handing over her ten pounds, twelve shillings and sixpence (I am still fairly certain that that was the exact cost of my Blacks down bag), had any inkling that she was not just allowing me two weeks' camping but fundamentally changing my life?

These philosophical reminiscences were soon cut short for, making my way over the series of rising steps that lead eventually to the summit, I realized that the weather was worsening rapidly, and my gaining height had meant that the rain was now turning to sleet and hail and falling with renewed force. I had met just one other person out that day, and the boot and paw prints in the patches of snow showed that he and his dog had been this way too. There was a sense of real achievement when I reached the summit at about three o'clock, having made good progress over the rough boulders that litter the final slope.

That construction workers have been on the summit is obvious, for a huge circular shelter has been built here, designed to offer protection no matter which way the wind blows. In good weather this summit offers good views, especially north to Torridon, but I could barely see 60 to 100 feet (18 to 30 m) ahead. It was also now very windy and cold on top, so having merely walked around the summit shelter I made my way down, noting that the weather improved only marginally (and that was mainly the temperature) as I lost height. Not until I was at the bealach did the mist partially clear, and then for only a minute or two. My sole companion during the last three hours had been a lone ptarmigan buffeted by the wind as it skimmed the surface of the hill.

As I arrived at the tent I was thankful I had had the sense to pitch it earlier and wondered if the following day would be any better. For weeks now the west had been experiencing the worst of the weather, and the unsettled conditions showed no signs of lifting. The rain and wind beat at the tent walls constantly throughout the long night, and later a local told me that this was 'certainly no night to be out in the mountains' but, as all hillgoers will know, exactly the opposite is true. There is a feeling of being close to nature and experiencing its elemental forces that comes from sleeping out on such nights. Predictably it is these memories that are still fresh in the mind, when those of sunnier times have merged to make an indistinct whole.

Maol Chean-dearg to Sgorr Ruadh

•

The following morning I had breakfasted by seven and was off by eight. The tops were still wreathed in mist and dampness hung in the air, but there was no doubt that an improvement looked possible. Following the well-defined stalkers' path I traversed Maol Chean-dearg, passing the isolated Loch Coire an Ruadh-staic. Looking back to An Ruadh-stac I was impressed by the wet, striated rock forming a broad diagonal band across the middle of the mountain. Ahead was the southern extremity of Beinn Damh, which from this direction presents a fine conical shape, and to its right the top of Liathach, ribbons of snow still lining the gullies. As I approached the dark waters of Loch an Eoin, I passed a number of small pools where numerous frogs were returning to mate. I also came across a herd of deer; some members ran off immediately while others watched me in what appeared inquisitive stillness.

At this loch my track met the path from Coulags which continues north-west to Annat, making a fine right of way from Glen Carron to Torridon. I now joined this path to continue my way around Loch an Eoin and south-east to the Bealach na Lice. In doing so I glanced up to Maol Chean-dearg's rocky northern slopes and felt that, the stalkers' paths notwithstanding, this is unspoilt, wild country. On the other side of the Bealach na Lice are panoramic views south down the glen that leads back to Coulags, with Loch Coire Fionnaraich immediately in front. For anyone undertaking a shorter journey, the path forks at a cairn by the stream, and a quick return to Coulags may be made. However, the land that lies ahead is in many ways even more impressive, and after a short break I continued along the path gaining height as I contoured around the southern side of Meall Dearg up to the Bealach Bàn and the northern extremity of Sgorr Ruadh. Clearly, no one had been this way for some time as my prints were the first ones in the old snow. Contouring around the mountain in this early spring weather was a magical experience, and nothing would have made me miss out on this impressive stretch of country that, today at least, was revelling in sombre grandeur. After a short rise of perhaps 330 feet (100 m) over an unnamed bealach and I was standing at the head of Coire Làir looking down this splendid glen with a choice of routes ahead.

It is possible immediately to stride out eastwards and, climbing steeply, follow a circuitous route onto Beinn Liath Mhór. Similarly, it is feasible to make an ascent of Sgorr Ruadh on the right. Although I had planned to ascend this fine mountain, together with its neighbour Fuar Tholl, time was of no consequence, and I chose to make my ascent further down the glen from the path that travels west to the saddle between their summits. Therefore, I wandered down the glen marvelling in the constantly changing craggy aspect of Sgorr Ruadh on my right and the emergence of Loch Coire Làir ahead.

Once I'd passed the loch, I dumped the rucksack, picked my way across the river (which can be very difficult in bad weather but was passable today) and started up the well-defined path leading up to Bealach Mór in the saddle separating Sgorr Ruadh (3156 feet/962 m) from its slightly lower neighbour, Fuar Tholl (2976 feet/907 m). Having walked around Sgorr Ruadh and been impressed by the rocky north-eastern sandstone cliffs, I eagerly made my way up to its summit. This is a mountain that has much to offer both the walker and the climber, and I was pleased to have walked around its base trying to distinguish prominent features like Raeburn's Buttress (named after the early rock pioneer Harold Raeburn) on its northern side followed by Academy Ridge and finally Robertson's Buttress on the north-eastern face which provided the earliest recorded easy climbing – if that is not a contradiction in terms for non-climbers! Now I was making my own ascent. At last I was rewarded with a fine view to Liathach and the other giants of Torridon before I retraced my steps. Pausing at the saddle and marvelling at the many small lochans, I had a quick rest before setting off for my final summit.

Fuar Tholl to Achnashellach or Coulags

•

Even my slight acquaintance with Gaelic placenames told me that Sgorr Ruadh translates as 'red peak', obviously taking its name from the sandstone buttresses rather than its quartzite ridges and screes. Today, after hours of heavy rain, the quartzite was beginning to sparkle, but the sandstone was still sombre and subdued. Fuar Tholl's name, equally descriptive but in a more elemental way, means 'cold hollow' or 'cold hole', and I could imagine easily how that had been acquired. I pictured settlers, perhaps centuries ago, talking, and one person asking another where he had been. After a wet day or two in the hills he – or she – would have pointed upwards and replied truthfully that he had been in that cold hollow!

I agree with the many people who rate this mountain as one of the country's finest Corbetts: those hills, gaining in popularity, are not as well known as the Munros but are more clearly defined. They are mountains between 2500 and 2999.9 feet (762 to 914 m) but they must have a drop of at least 500 feet (152 m) between themselves and any other mountain, which results in their usually being more clearly separated than is the case with Munros. They number 220 in all and are named after John Rooke Corbett who, in spite of working in Bristol, was a keen

PREVIOUS PAGES: ON MAOL CHEAN-DEARG LOOKING TOWARDS FUAR THOLL

•

member of the Scottish Mountaineering Club and in 1930 was the second person to complete all the Munros and tops. For anyone starting to bag the Corbetts, Fuar Tholl is a good early acquisition.

The mountain was also making a fitting conclusion to my walk as I climbed upwards in one of Scotland's grandest settings. I headed into Coire Mainnrichean, keeping the awesome Mainreachan Buttress on my right, and completed the final steep heave to arrival at the col on the summit ridge. It remained only to make the short journey north-eastwards to the trig point and shelter that mark the very top. After a few photographs hopefully taken in the improving light and a quick exploration, it was time to make my descent and think about returning home. Most people will have undoubtedly come here by private car and parked at Coulags, so an obvious return route is to drop off the southern flank, passing over Carn Eididh and continuing down the nose back to the road. However, I had a train to catch and they have never run that frequently in these parts!

The route down to Achnashellach station is outstanding in summer but enjoyable at any time of year. I kept stopping to look back at the mountains that had dominated my thoughts for the last two days wishing that my time here could be longer. Following the River Làir, I marvelled at the Scots pines, remnants of the ancient forest, and at the river itself as it made its way through a succession of enticing pools and waterfalls. Only a final diversion through a forestry plantation together with some unsightly felling reminded me that we have still much to learn about the proper use of our precious landscape. It seems that so often much of what we do is just plain clumsy and makes an unnecessary scar on the landscape. No one would claim that forestry is a clean business, and in isolated areas like this it can bring much needed employment. It is a pity that the felling of mature trees leaves such an unsightly scar. Of course, I do not doubt that when the railway that runs alongside was originally built, some people probably expressed very similar sentiments. Yet with the passing of the years it has blended into the landscape and now appears an integral part of it.

At one time the Highland Railway Company operated the line from Inverness in its own somewhat eccentric way but today's operation is more efficient. Some people say such rural services are unreliable and inconvenient; this may be true but more often than not they work extremely well, especially considering their remoteness. Today the 17.56 was running on time, and I spent the first part of my return journey looking at the passing hills and thinking of other long walks I had still to do in this area. As I did so I recalled what a psychologist friend had once said to me. 'Leaving something unfinished,' she mused, 'is a subconscious desire for returning.' That is particularly true of the mountains around here.

The hills of the Coulin Forest and Loch Torridon from Beinn Liath Mhor

•

CHAPTER TEN

BEINN DEARG AND EASTER ROSS

A MOUNTAIN ODYSSEY

•

Richard Else

A three-day exploration in a remote mountain landscape

MAP: *OS 1:50 000 Sheet 20*
START AND FINISH: *The Craigs at the head of Strathcarron. Grid Ref: 473909*
LENGTH: *About 38 miles (58 km)*
APPROXIMATE TIME: *3 days*
TERRAIN: *Remote mountain country where careful navigation is required in poor visibility*
ACCOMMODATION: *A choice of places at which to stay in such villages as Ardgay and Bonar Bridge. Away from the east coast accommodation is limited*

As I travel north along the A835 from Inverness to Ullapool my attention is always drawn eastwards to the compact group of mountains centred around Beinn Dearg at the head of Gleann na Sguaib. The view from the road gives a tantalizing glimpse of these hills, and while I suspect that most walkers come here for the five Munros in this area – Beinn Dearg, Cona Mheall, Meall nan Ceapraichean, Eididh nan Clach Geala and Seana Bhraigh – there are many other reasons for visiting this region. It provides, for example, the shortest west-to-east crossing in Scotland, connecting the head of Loch Broom with the Dornoch Firth at Ardgay. In fact, I had been thinking of undertaking this traverse (but from east to west) and making use of public transport to do so. I thought the train to Ardgay followed by the post-bus or a taxi into Strathcarron would work, and I would return to Inverness by bus. In the event I escaped from the office on Friday morning for a long weekend and, as I would be returning on a Sunday, I took my

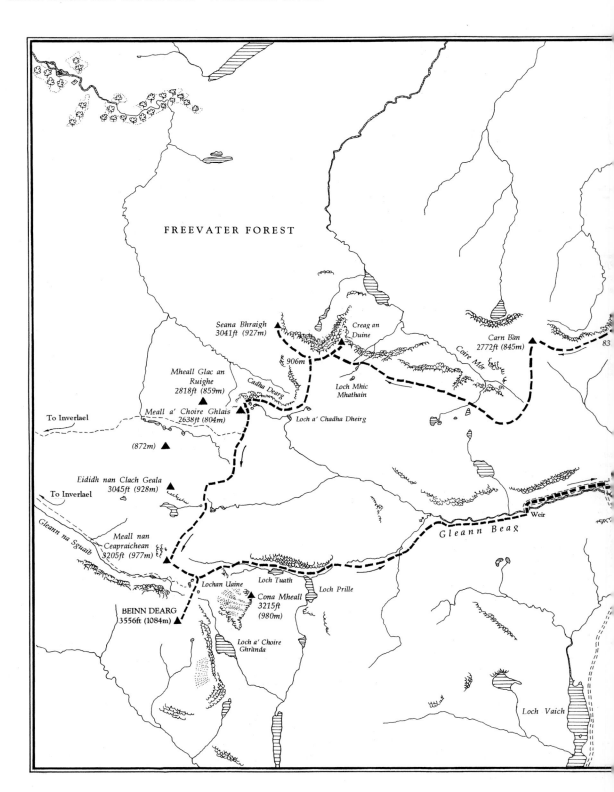

FREEVATER FOREST

Seana Bhraigh
3041ft (927m)

Creag an
Duine

906m

Carn Bàn
2772ft (845m)

83

Coire Mòr

Mheall Glac an
Ruighe
2818ft (859m)

Cadha Dearg

Loch Mhic
Mhathain

To Inverlael

Meall a' Choire Ghlais
2638ft (804m)

Loch a' Chadha Dheirg

(872m)

Eididh nan Clach Geala
3045ft (928m)

To Inverlael

Weir

Gleann na Sguaib

Gleann Beag

Meall nan
Ceapraichean
3205ft (977m)

Loch Tuath

Lochan Uaine

Loch Prille

Cona Mheall
3215ft
(980m)

BEINN DEARG
3556ft (1084m)

Loch a' Choire
Ghrànda

Loch Vaich

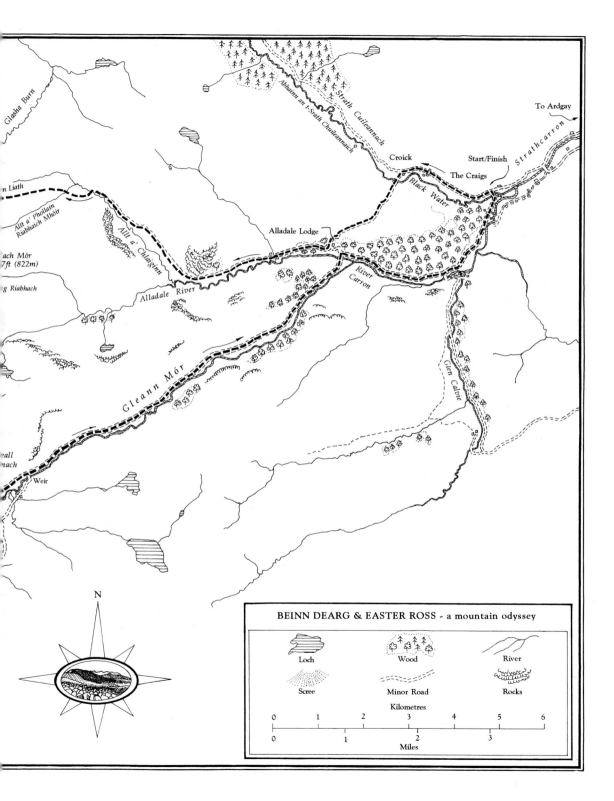

Glasha Burn

n Liath

Allt a' Phollain
Riabhaich Mhòr

ach Mòr
7ft (822m)

g Riabhach

Allt a' Chlaiginn

Alladale River

Gleann Mór

eall
nach

Weir

Abhainn an t-Srath Chuileannaich

Strath Cuileannach

Croick

The Craigs

Start/Finish

To Ardgay

Strathcarron

Black Water

Alladale Lodge

River
Carron

Glen Calvie

N

BEINN DEARG & EASTER ROSS - a mountain odyssey

Loch	Wood	River
Scree	Minor Road	Rocks

Kilometres

| 0 | 1 | 2 | 3 | 4 | 5 | 6 |

| 0 | 1 | 2 | 3 |

Miles

car instead. This imposed its own discipline, and after some poring over the map I decided an approach from the east would allow me to discover much more of this remote part of Easter Ross. My route would involve leaving the Land Rover by The Craigs at the head of Strathcarron which is virtually the end of the public road. From here I would walk via Croick with its few buildings and church, before following the track to Alladale Lodge and then up the Alladale River and Allt a' Chlaiginn. I planned to gain the high ground at Bodach Mór, from where I would start a circuit of the high tops, taking in Carn Bàn, Seana Bhraigh, Meall nan Ceapraichean and finally Beinn Dearg. With an extra day it would have been possible to take in all the summits, but I needed to allow time for a long walk out down Gleanns Beag and Mór which would give me a different perspective on this landscape.

I was delighted to have managed to add an extra day to the weekend, and I drove down Strathcarron thinking that there is nothing better than to know that other people are working when I am escaping to the hills. This glen is still well populated today and is highly prized for its fishing. Crofts, cottages and a number of well-maintained lodges line this charming glen which, at its western end, is a focal point for

Looking south from Seana Bhraigh, one of the remotest hills of Scotland

•

a number of other subsidiary glens. While these have either private tracks or stalkers' paths, it is a blessing that no public roads run through this area, making it an ideal place for wild walking and real exploration. I parked by the old-fashioned telephone box at The Craigs, my mood reflected in the blue sky and spring sunshine. I planned to enjoy my trip through this glaciated landscape, with its deep U-shaped valleys, extensive cliffs and wild, remote lochs. The mile to Croick is along a tarred road but already the bustle of Strathcarron has been left behind. I had long wanted to visit the church here, which is interesting both on its own account and for the role it played in the Highland Clearances. Designed by Thomas Telford, it was completed in 1827 as one of 43 churches established and financed by Parliament as a thank you for victory in the Napoleonic Wars. Visiting the church today, I was impressed by the simplicity of the design both inside and out, yet like almost all visitors I had come to look at the east window of the church. For it was here, on the individual panes of glass that make up the window, that the tenants of the area scratched their plaintive messages during the Clearances of 1845. After successfully fighting eviction for three years they finally succumbed and were cleared from their homes in Glen Calvie, where they had lived for generations. Prior to leaving the glen for the last time they took shelter in the churchyard and wrote their sad messages on the glass. I was moved by what had happened at Croick and left the church in sombre mood. Recently, sensing the public mood for a tangible measure of land reform within Scotland and with the establishment of a National Parliament within sight, the Scottish Landowners' Federation had tried to apologize for the Highland Clearances. Whether it is possible to simply apologize in this way for an enforced exodus of a whole section of society who were shipped off like cattle to distant countries is a debatable point, but in any event the move seems to have backfired on the SLF amid calls for true land reform and not simply a belated apology for historical acts that changed the whole face of the Highlands.

I was thinking about these events – past and recent – as I started walking down the side of the churchyard and crossed over the Abhainn an t-Srath Chuileannaich, which becomes the Black Water shortly after passing the church. I was following a little-used path, virtually unmarked on the ground, that would take me south-west to Alladale Lodge. I do not doubt that the splendour of the scenery and my exploration of this landscape would soon have driven any thoughts about the Clearances and present-day views on land ownership firmly from my mind if it had not been for a number of events that happened in quick succession. I reached the bealach separating Strath Cuileannach from Glen Alladale only to be greeted by a recent electrified deer-fence that appeared to run for miles. Although a stile has been built over the fence where the track crosses it, the track at this point has virtually vanished and it may well take some finding (in fact it is in a slight depression and probably to the east of where it might be expected) and no alternatives appear to be offered. In recent years the use of such widespread deer-fencing has been justified with the argument that it allows the native woodland to regenerate and on these occasions its use has been supported by Scottish Natural Heritage. However, the use of such fencing as that running along before me, where it stretches almost as far as the eye can see, has not been without controversy and a number of distinguished natural historians have argued that such fencing has undesirable side-effects (not least the number of protected birds that fly into it and are killed) and that it evades the real problem of the excessive number of deer. Of course, the latter argument is often an unpalatable one to landowners, who rely on revenue from stalking parties. In any event the widespread use of deer-fencing is, without doubt, a gross visual intrusion on the landscape and one that perhaps deserves a more considered debate.

Once past Alladale Lodge I turned westwards and started to walk up the glen, but almost immediately I came across a gate with the following notice:

Alladale Estate
No unauthorised access for hill walking, camping or cycling during the hunting season
(July 1st to Feb 15th), at other times please contact estate office.

This was one of the least welcoming signs (to put it at its most charitable!) I had seen in a long time and one that serves to show how wide the gulf remains between some landowners and other hill-folk. While such notices may have always been unacceptable, they were more common at one time, but now they are totally out of keeping with present-day attitudes. Moreover, a notice such as this ignores both the recent Concordat on access to the hills (which was signed by a number of bodies representing a wide variety of interests, including the Scottish Landowners' Federation, Scottish Countryside Activities Council, Scottish Natural Heritage, National Farmers' Union of Scotland and Ramblers' Association, Scotland) and the traditional right to roam that exists within Scotland. Some people may have criticized the Concordat as being too vaguely worded, especially when one considers the Letterewe Accord (mentioned in the first edition of *Wilderness Walks*) but in any event while such notices exist, the sad truth is that the Concordat is not worth the paper it is written on. The idea of being allowed no access for the majority of the year and having to contact the estate office at all other times is so at odds with current thinking as to be scarcely believable.

If this notice is offensive to walkers, I hope it will also give a similar message to other landowners. In fact, it is all too easy to point the accusing finger at private landowners, yet in some (perhaps even many) cases they have been among the most enlightened. Whatever the original background, Paul Van Vlissingen put his signature to the Letterewe Accord long before Scottish Natural Heritage produced its own Concordat. Indeed, where I live the local stalker puts up a friendly notice at the end of the main stalking season thanking all walkers for their cooperation. The real problem, in my opinion, with private ownership is that one is never quite sure about the future of the land. The present owner may be excellent, but what about those who follow in successive generations? On the other hand there are also examples of public land ownership that leave much to be desired. Standing by the Alladale notice I realized that it caused offence in more ways than one. First, most people would accept that the bulk of the stalking season runs from around 20 August to 20 October and during this period walkers should be most aware of the needs of landowners. The idea that the 'hunting season' runs for nearly eight months, from 1 July to 15 February, and that walkers should be excluded during the whole of this time is a nonsense. Similarly, there is no suggestion that contacting the estate will result in alternative routes being offered. No, the subtext of this sign is that the Alladale land is private and that visitors are

ABOVE: SEANA BHRAIGH FROM THE SUBSIDIARY TOP OF CREAG AN DUINE

RIGHT: THE UGLY SCAR OF THE NEWLY CONSTRUCTED ESTATE ROAD

•

discouraged. I would be happy to say that this was an old sign and that attitudes had changed, but sadly that appears not to be the case. The sign was fairly recent, its meaning unambiguous. I was already forming a clear view about the Alladale Estate, and this was confirmed as I ignored their kind offer to contact the estate office and made my way down the glen. This beautiful glen now has an enormous scar right down its middle where a newly constructed road has been made. Doubtless it is well made and will bed into its surroundings in time, but work of this kind is always a shock in such a remote and unspoilt landscape.

Crossing the Allt a' Chlaiginn and the cumbersomely named Allt a' Phollain Riabhaich Mhóir (not surprisingly unnamed on the 1:50 000 map) I tried to enjoy the natural landscape rather than the human scars inflicted on it. Fortunately, not long afterwards I found more pleasant sights. I walked alongside the stream and watched it plunge through a succession of miniature gorges, cascading between them in a series of small but powerful waterfalls.

As so often in Scotland, the walking underfoot became easier as I gained height, and walking up the slope known as Glun Liath I soon gained enough altitude to be able to see over the deep glens. It came as a surprise to discover excellent visibility and clear, sharp views in all directions, with numerous mountains breaking the skyline. Without any warning I was presented with a stunning panorama of northern hills, including Ben Kilbreck and Ben Hope due north, the bulk of Ben More Assynt and beyond it the hills of Reay Forest just to the west of north and, once I had gained more height, the outlines of Canisp, Suilven, Cul Mor, Stac Pollaidh and Ben Mór Coigach away to the north-west.

I arrived on the summit of Bodach Mór some time between five and six o'clock, having been encouraged during the final few minutes by the view that simultaneously extended eastwards to the Dornoch Firth and the North Sea beyond and westwards to the Summer Isles, The Minch and, on the skyline, the distinctive outline of Lewis in the Outer Hebrides. I had difficulty in finding words that adequately expressed the real joy I was feeling, but I now left the summit with an unfettered step to savour the easy ridge walk on short turf and stones, my eye always attracted to the brilliant quartzite boulders that dotted the plateau. To my right the ground fell away in a series of cliffs to the deep coire occupied by the Glasha Burn. My plan was to contour around these cliffs, and I took in Creag Riabhach without much notice before passing point 837 and walking off its slope to the bealach between it and Carn Bàn. I planned to camp here for the night and was pleased to find there was no shortage of water. I put up my tent noting with approval the red sky that had progressively formed over the last half-hour or so. During this time I had been thinking about the psychology of finding shelter and how the simple act of erecting a tent had on many previous occasions altered my mood from one of nervousness to security. I remembered, for example, an occasion on Skye when I put up the tent in darkness during a howling storm and crawled inside with a sense of relief that was complete once the stove was assembled and roaring away. On other occasions, again in winter, I had awoken to find a new fall of snow and the temperature well below freezing, but in the comfort of my sleeping-bag I had been blissfully unaware of the changed conditions.

Tonight there was virtually no wind, in spite of my being above 2300 feet (701 m), and a full moon made my satisfaction complete as I watched it slowly appear then disappear behind the high clouds. With such a good omen, I knew this evening would be remembered for a long time and, although I turned in with reluctance, not long afterwards I was sound asleep.

Saturday started lazily with breakfast and coffee in my sleeping-bag, and when I emerged from the tent at around half-past seven visibility was reduced, and the day was dull and sombre – but at least it was dry with a hint that things might even improve. With some satisfaction I noticed that the weather was worse on more distant hills, where rain showers were obvious.

Carn Bàn to Beinn Dearg

•

My own morning started with an easy ascent of Carn Bàn followed by walking south along the summit plateau. When I'd planned this trip I had thought there might be two difficult sections, of which the next would be one. But my worries were largely unfounded. It is important to travel south from Carn Bàn to avoid a long and wasteful descent, and eventually I crossed over an area of peat hags and streams and followed an easy ramp that took me towards the steep cliffs on the southern face of Coire Mór. I picked my way over the rough ground much as the mood took me, sometimes looking down the deep chasm into the head of Coire Mór, approximately 1300 feet (400 m) lower, while on other occasions I temporarily left the cliffs to avoid some of the deepest incisions in the land caused by the streams cutting deep into the soft peat. Surprisingly, the journey was not too boggy, and keeping to the easiest line was a simple process of pausing every 20 minutes or so and deciding on the next section. I was impressed by virtually all that I saw and discovered that such scenes were as likely to be found among the lochans and their streams as in the wider picture of Coire Mór, which is undoubtedly spectacular, and beyond.

I had adopted a *laissez-faire* attitude to my weekend, and being unconcerned with acquiring or repeating Munros had decided to divide my time equally between all aspects of this fine landscape. I now followed a line that easily led from Loch Mhic Mhathain (unmarked on the 1: 50 000 map but at grid reference 299869) to a bealach between Creag an Duine and point 906. From here it is a quick ascent to the former and the sharp, pointed top An Sgurr (named in guidebooks but unacknowledged on even the 1: 25 000 OS map) before steps are retraced for the easy walking

Seana Bhraigh rising steeply beyond the great trench of the Cadha Dearg

•

that leads to the summit of Seana Bhraigh, where I stopped for a well-earned lunch.

Seana Bhraigh, along with A' Mhaighdean in Letterewe, is usually considered the most inaccessible of the mainland Munros, even the most direct approach from the west necessitating a long walk in. My own meandering route from the east was even longer, but over lunch I considered its merits. It had, for instance, given me time to appreciate these fine hills and the remote landscape they are set in. Similarly, my route illustrates the benefits of a multi-day trip when itineraries can be more relaxed, diversions can be undertaken at will and, most important, there is simply more time to understand and appreciate all that I see. I was in no hurry to finish my lunch as I absorbed the tremendous views north-west to the Coigach hills. Equally, I felt this summit was particularly deserved, especially when I recalled my journey through this jumbled, deserted landscape. I packed my rucksack watching two ptarmigans fly across the summit plateau and thought about the way ahead. Almost due south was the prominent bulk of Beinn Dearg, still ribboned in late snow, and the twisted cone of its neighbour, Cona Mheall. Together they defined my route, with Beinn Dearg literally and metaphorically the high point of my trip.

With the unpredictability of the weather together with conditions underfoot, I had been unwilling to make precise plans but so far I had achieved all my objectives. In one way I felt uneasy about this, believing that the mountains are not merely for our recreation: usually, I am happiest when plans have to be modified, and itineraries planned at home take on the sense of a real adventure. Similarly, I have an intense dislike of all plans. Of course, plans are an absolute necessity in most aspects of our lives, serving to prevent a descent into chaos, but I think they can also stifle creativity, prevent really original thought and bind us with a set of preconceptions. In reality, I am happiest when the inevitable plans serve only as a guide to be discarded, modified or replaced.

As if to illustrate the point about the fallibility of such preconceptions, I started on the journey down from Seana Bhraigh and around the steep cliffs above Cadha Dearg. This was one of the many magnificent places on this long walk with streams running under my feet before they immediately plunged some 1150 feet (350 m) into the glen far below. I had anticipated that the next part of the walk would be arduous, with hard going under foot, but in fact it was somewhat easier than the ground between Carn Bàn and Seana Bhraigh. With no ambition to climb all the tops in the area, I took a course that continued to contour around the head of Cadha Dearg, where I was rewarded by a constantly changing perspective that never failed to keep my attention.

The next section may pose problems of navigation in bad visibility, but I encountered no difficulties as I followed a route that took me south and away from the cliffs. I passed three upland lochans that revealed themselves one at a time, traversed the plateau to the east of Meall a' Choire Ghlais (not named on the 1: 50 000 map), passing the end of the path that leads up from Inverlael, before contouring around Eididh nan Clach Geala. Looking up to the summit, which was over half a mile away, I saw the first other people of the day and watched for a moment as two figures began their descent to the north as the rain finally arrived. Bad weather seemed to have affected all the other hills apart from this particular small group for most of the day; now it was my turn to get out the jacket and button up as the rain started with a seriousness that announced it was not going to be a brief passing shower.

Over the years every walker acquires a set of clothing and equipment that best suits his or her particular needs. With some items, like tents and shell garments, this is relatively simple and a trade-off is made between functionality, weight and, most important, price. I have always felt it odd that while most gear is well specified, even over-specified, little attention has been given to some basic requirements. Take the question of maps as a simple illustration. I have a deep-seated dislike of map cases which, in consequence, has seen many good maps ruined over the years and, in talking to other walkers, found this to be a common experience. There have been attempts to produce laminated maps but often these were bulky and difficult to use on the hills. I had thought the problem a simple one but probably insoluble until I discovered, a couple of years ago, the maps laminated by Chartech in the Peak District. By using their own techniques (and offering a couple of alternatives) and the simple expedient of folding the map in half prior to lamination, they have managed to achieve a water-proof map that is not like a folded concertina.

I wove my way up the narrow path (the first of the day) that led to Meal nan Ceapraichean with the rain sheeting down. The rain was still falling as I arrived at the stony summit but that did not spoil my enjoyment, for this is a fine top that affords good close-up views of the northern face of Beinn Dearg, which now looked particularly stark.

I wondered how long the rain would continue as I watched the mist circle around Beinn Dearg. This is one of my favourite hills, and I wanted to be on its summit able to admire the fine views it affords. As a consequence I descended the south-eastern slope of Meall nan Ceapraichean and pitched my tent by the lochan (named as Lochan Uaine on the 1: 25 000 map) between both peaks. Most of my clothing was wet from the downpour, so I settled into the tent and made a brew and a meal while relishing this high camp. Just after six o'clock the weather started to improve, so I set off for Beinn Dearg following the imposing wall that leads from the bealach to a few hundred yards short of the summit. I was making my way up wet rocks and soft snow, and in less than 45 minutes was standing next to the substantial summit cairn marvelling at the sun as it broke through the cloud to illuminate first one part of this crumpled land-scape and then another. The quality of light was phenomenal and held me captivated. Standing there, I felt a warm glow of achievement, thrilled at how my long weekend was turning out. Gradually, I was aware of something else, the exhilarating realization that this was my best summit for years, with a wild landscape spread out before me and a view that encompassed many mountains I had previously climbed. An assortment of memories came out of many remote corners of my brain as I continued to stand there.

BEINN DEARG AND THE FANNICHS FROM EIDIDH NAN CLACH GEALA

•

Then another incoming storm finally told me it was time to leave, and I started my return to the tent uplifted in body and spirit.

Shortly after my return, a final storm developed that continued all night, bringing high winds and heavy rain that left the ground sodden. I would have liked to have visited Cona Mheall that morning, but the mountain was wreathed in mist and in any case I had a walk-out of around 15 miles (24 km) which I did not want to hurry. In truth, I had wondered if I would really enjoy such a long walk back, which was really occasioned only because I had used my car. Yet the journey eastwards is no way inferior to what has gone before. The route includes high lochs like Tuath and Prille which have a remote, wild charm. As I glanced back, the mountains showed changing perspectives, and once Gleann Beag is reached the walking becomes easy and the miles start to glide by. I explored briefly the water catchment works half-way down the

glen before contouring around the base of Meall Dionach and into Gleann Mór. The morning's rain had now given way to warm sunshine. Eventually, I walked into the woodlands at the far end of the glen and emerged by a gate just before the River Carron. Once again I was forcibly reminded of the antics of the Alladale Estate by the following notice which, in its entirety, reads:

Alladale Estate

Deer culling, together with conservation projects in conjunction with Scottish Natural Heritage, take place on this estate. In everyone's interests and for safety reasons, please contact the keeper (Tel 01863 755338) before visiting. Thank you for your help. While red disc displayed shooting in progress.

By now I was absolutely seething at the bare-faced cheek of this sign, especially as it sought to implicate Scottish Natural Heritage in the desire to keep everyone out. Just what, I kept asking myself, were 'everyone's interests' and exactly what 'safety reasons' prevailed here that were not evident throughout the remainder of the Scottish Highlands? I also admired the ploy of trying to appear helpful by providing a phone number when the nearest phone box is three miles (five km) back along the track; in fact, exactly where I had parked my car. During these remaining few miles I formulated a plan.

During the next few days I discovered fellow walkers who had been so intimidated by the notices that they had not even bothered to set foot on the estate. I rang Dave Morris of the Ramblers' Association, who listened to my experiences with growing incredulity. Then I started calling a number of organizations, including the Scottish Landowners' Federation and Scottish Natural Heritage.

Perhaps most interesting from a walkers' viewpoint was the response of the Scottish Landowners' Federation: they simply refused to answer two simple queries. I wanted to know whether the Alladale Estate were members of the SLF and, secondly, who owned the estate. The latter information is available in Andy Wightman's excellent book *Who Owns Scotland*, but I was anxious to check if this were up to date. Thinking my query was a general one from a member of the public, the SLF claimed they were unable to answer either question, saying that such information was confidential under the Data Protection Act. A later conversation with their director was no more satisfactory, for while the SLF encourages their members to follow the Concordat it cannot bind them to do so. Of course, the SLF could alter its terms of registration to make membership information more freely available, just as it could take measures to deal with members who pay little attention to the Concordat. I was left feeling that its signature on the current Concordat has little real value and that it is one of the more secretive organizations in Scotland. The position of Scottish Natural Heritage is more difficult. While they are in their own words 'aware' of the offending signs and, of course, the phrase in the Concordat that reads, 'Any local restrictions on access should be essential for the needs of management, should be fully explained, and for the minimum period and area required', they appear stuck between a rock and a hard place. On the one hand they must be sensitive to the needs of the Estate but they must also recognize and respond to the mood of the times. Whether, with hindsight, their remit is too broad and cannot ultimately be fulfilled is, perhaps, a matter for debate.

After my round of telephone calls I was left with the clear impression that the Concordat is in need of further work and that, while many estates are to be applauded in their attitude to hill-walkers, others still give an impression that walkers and other hill-folk are not particularly welcome.

CHAPTER ELEVEN

REAY FOREST

A CELEBRATION OF REMOTENESS

•

Richard Else

A two-day mountain trek in outstanding mountain countryside

MAP: *OS 1:50 000 Sheet 9*
START: *Laxford Bridge. Grid Ref: 237469.*
FINISH: *Just north of Rhiconich on the A838. Grid Ref: 266529*
LENGTH: *Approximately 20 miles (32 km)*
APPROXIMATE TIME: *2 days, but can be extended to make a longer trip*
TERRAIN: *A journey through wild, remote mountain country*
ACCOMMODATION: *In this area accommodation is limited. In addition to a number of
guest-houses, the Rhiconich Hotel and The Old School Restaurant and Guest-house at
Inshegra (on the road to Kinlochbervie) can be highly recommended. Both offer extremely good facilities
and excellent food and make walkers very welcome*

I have often been curious about what foreign tourists planning a holiday in the
far north-west of Scotland have made of Laxford Bridge. Seeing the name
marked prominently on the map at the junction of two A-roads and at the
head of a great sea loch, I wonder if they have thought of it as a good place at
which to spend the night, to do a little shopping or, perhaps, to stop for a
coffee and snack. Imagine their surprise then, when actually arriving there they find
that Laxford Bridge is, if you ignore a couple of estate cottages, just, well, Laxford
Bridge! Like so many places in this part of the world, appearances are deceptive, and
the map has to be read in an entirely different way. Settlements that appear to be
quite large have perhaps just a shop or a small hotel for the traveller, and such placenames are often given to a few homes. This very quality of isolation is, of course, the
real attraction of this landscape and one that brings a few devotees back year after
year. Among those comparatively few walkers who get north of Inverness, even

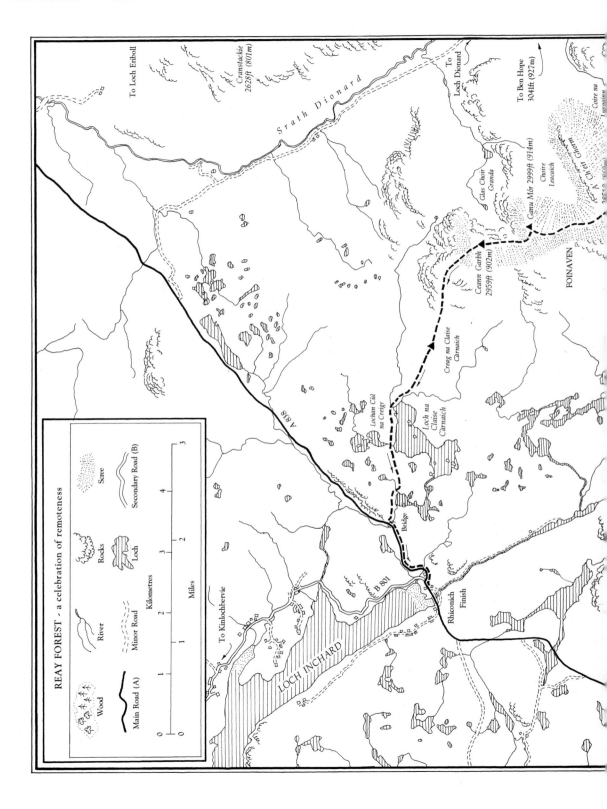

To Loch Eriboll

Cranstackie
2628ft (801m)

Srath Dionard

To
Loch Dionard

To Ben Hope
3041ft (927m)

Glas Choir
Granda

Ganu Mór 2999ft (914m)

Choire
Leacaich

A'Chir Ghorm

Coire na
Lugeainn

FOINAVEN

Ceann Garbh
2959ft (902m)

Creag na Claise
Càrnaich

A 838

Lochan Cùl
na Creige

Loch na
Claise
Càrnaich

Bridge

B 801

Rhiconich
Finish

To Kinlochbervie

LOCH INCHARD

REAY FOREST - a celebration of remoteness

Wood	River	Scree
Rocks	Loch	Secondary Road (B)
Main Road (A)	Minor Road	

Kilometres

0   1   2   3   4   5

Miles

0   1   2   3

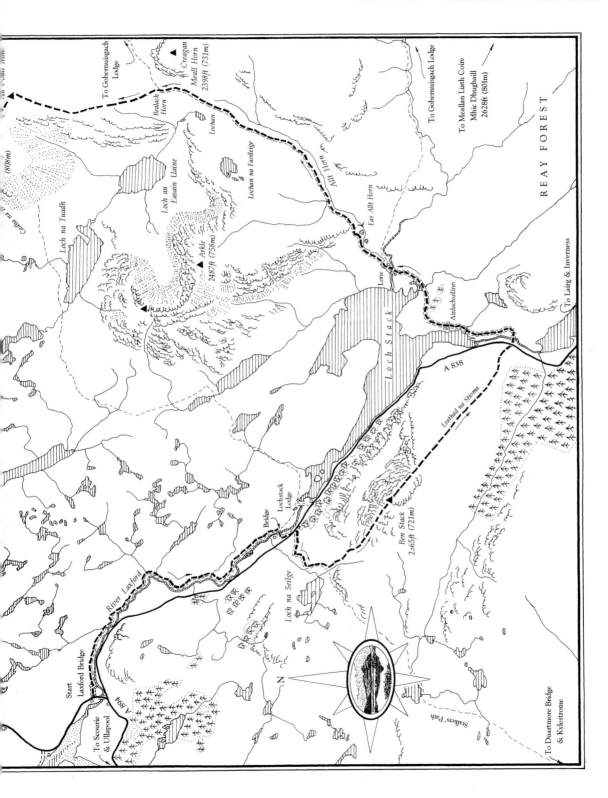

To Gobernuisgach Lodge

Creagan
Meall Horn
2398ft (731m)

Bealach
Horn

Lochan

Lochan na Faoileige

Loch an
Easain Uaine

Allt Horn

Lus Allt Horn

To Gobernuisgach Lodge

To Meallan Liath Coire
Mhic Dhughaill
2628ft (801m)

REAY FOREST

(808m)

Loch na Tuadh

Caoinne na Faoileige

Arkle
2487ft (758m)

Lone

To Lairg & Inverness

Airdachuilinn

Loch Stack

A 838

Leathad na Stioma

Ben Stack
2.65ft (721m)

Bridge

Lochstack
Lodge

River Laxford

Loch na Seilge

N

Start

Laxford Bridge

To Scourie
& Ullapool

A 894

Stalker's Path

To Duartmore Bridge
& Kylestrome

fewer manage to explore this least-visited part of the Scottish mainland. Many simply make a quick dash up Ben Hope and Ben Klibreck to claim their two Munros before heading back south for other three-thousanders. In doing so they ignore a landscape and seascape that have no equal in the British Isles and no apology should be necessary for including two fine but contrasting expeditions in this far outpost (see Chapter 12). After undertaking the routes in this and the next chapter, any keen walker should be hooked!

It is possible to define carefully the far north-west, but my own imprecise definition is based on what I feel in my heart and see with my eyes every time I make this pilgrimage. Once I am north of Ullapool and west of Lairg (both veritable metropolises by the standards in these parts), I know I have arrived. Even for someone like myself who now lives in the Scottish Highlands, this is still over two hours from my home and in this part of the world the south does not mean London but Inverness! In this region the number of communities of any size does not even reach double figures (although most of them offer genuine hospitality and provide a high standard of facilities for visitors) in an area of roughly 1000 square miles (2590 square km). Outside the short tourist season (late May to early September) many places are closed and good accommodation is as likely to be offered by isolated hotels and b&bs as by those within villages. Using public transport requires detailed planning but is not the impossibility it might be thought (especially by an imaginative combination of train, bus and post-bus) and its unhurried pace forms an appropriate introduction to the area.

Many special qualities make Sutherland a particular favourite of mine, but they all stem from the landscape and the way humans have interacted with it over the centuries. As much seascape as landscape, Sutherland's characteristic features are the large sea lochs, often making great fingers inland; equally impressive are the freshwater ones. Then there are what seem like innumerable lochans occupying nearly every depression and glinting in the sun like a thousand priceless jewels. (Incidentally, to get a real sense of just how many of these there are, take a look at one of the Ordnance Survey's 1:25 000 Pathfinder sheets where the true extent of water cover is striking.) Finally, there are the hills themselves; their attraction is less to do with their height than with their situation: a feeling of complete remoteness and, most important of all, the fact that they rise straight up virtually from sea-level.

All these features result from the complicated geological structure of the area. Lewisian gneiss, the oldest rock in Britain, dating from some 1500 to 2000 million years ago and characteristically grey, is much in evidence. It is often overlaid by Torridonian sandstone (a mere 800 million years old) together with the more recent Cambrian quartzite.

Today, tourism supplements the traditional crofting in communities like Scourie, while Kinlochbervie is an important fishing port with much development to both port and village in recent years (including an impressive new school). The inland areas were once the traditional hunting forests of the Lords of Reay, who were the chiefs of Clan Mackay. Today, the Westminster family are the largest single landowners, and much of this area is still kept for the sporting activities of stalking and fishing.

Outside the stalking season there is no shortage of fine multi-day expeditions that take in the high tops together with a number of routes that make use of high-level stalkers' paths and these can be equally satisfying, especially if the weather is poor. Such routes include a number of traverses that meet at Gobernuisgach Lodge (grid reference 436418) and are marked on the 1:50 000 map. However, one problem with many routes is the need for transport at one end or the other. It was partly with a desire to minimize this need that I planned the following route, which not only takes in what many would consider the most outstanding mountain in the area but also has a wealth of other features.

Laxford Bridge to Ben Stack

I have always found that this part of Scotland seems to make its own weather, so any general forecast is exactly that and too general to be of any real use. I have known superb weather here, with bright clear days, when the rest of Scotland is under cloud and rain. Unfortunately, the opposite can also be true. Often fine days on the mountains can follow the most unpromising beginnings, and if ever the maxim that 'you should just go and rub your nose in the weather' is true, then it is in Sutherland.

This walk can begin either from Rhiconich (especially useful if staying at the hotel there) or from Laxford Bridge, which has yet to introduce yellow lines and parking meters. The first option entails begging a lift or using the early-morning post-bus, neither of which should present any problems.

I harboured a quizzical feeling as I started to walk along the path from Laxford Bridge which follows the northern side of the River Laxford. For the first mile or so upstream the path and the A838 run side by side separated only by the river itself. In the heart of England such a walk would rarely be pleasant, but the A838 from Lairg must be one of the smallest A-roads in Britain. Here it is more often than not simply a single-track road with passing-places – a sure sign of walking in a different world! Incidentally, numerous stretches of the original A894 north of Ullapool, with its narrow bridges, provide evidence of an age when the motor car was a rarity and this area was truly isolated and journey times would be measured in days, not hours. Then you queued for the ferry at Kylesku where today you follow the sweeping arch

SUNSET OVER THE LOCH-SPLATTERED LANDSCAPE AROUND LOCH INCHARD

of the modern bridge. The late Paul Nunn, an old friend of mine and both a talented climber (President of the British Mountaineering Council at the time of his death) and a fine historian, with a quirkiness that typified much of what he said, worked out that until recent road improvements were made it was quicker to travel from Sheffield to climb in California than on the outcrops of the far north-west. Yet long journey times did not prevent Paul and his many friends from putting up a number of bold first ascents throughout the whole of this area.

The path I was following is obviously little used but well maintained; as with many such paths hereabouts, such maintenance shows their importance to the sporting fraternity. Similarly, the River Laxford is known for its good salmon and there was much evidence of this in the three miles (four km) I walked alongside it. I passed by what can best be described as a fishing pier that must have been a major undertaking when built. Constructed of concrete and steel, a column supports an extension that allows the pool below to be fished in a most civilized way. Further along is a wire ropeway with bosun's chair that allows an easy crossing – again without getting wet feet!

Just short of Lochstack Lodge is a more traditional bridge some three planks wide supported by an iron rail which allows walkers an easy crossing. On the southern side of the A838 Ben Stack, in spite of its modest height, dominates the landscape every bit as much as Arkle and Foinaven do on the opposite side. I was hoping to make ascents of both Ben Stack and Foinaven but they were by no means the only highlights I was anticipating on this trip. In this particular area the chances of meeting other walkers are, outside July and early August, quite slim and that sense of solitude is strengthened by the features of this landscape. As I walked along, words like 'hewn', 'rough' and 'stark' came most quickly to mind. Yet this is not a bleak, threatening landscape, and for a long time I have puzzled as to why this is the case. Personally I find the place one of great peacefulness and offering a rare beauty. I think two factors contribute to this feeling: first, land, sea and sky come together in a particularly striking way that I do not think is found in many places other than the Outer Isles, and secondly the region has a quite breathtaking quality of light that has real translucence and depth. If that sounds somewhat fanciful, just stand at the head of one of the numerous lochs watching the sunset, or from higher ground look out across this wild environment when penetrating rays of sun chase the rain clouds away.

Today, as I walked the very short distance east along the road I kept glancing upwards to Arkle with Foinaven behind and noticed how the mist kept encircling just their very tops. Compared with the weather further south, which was full of rain, this was a real treat. My first objective was Ben Stack, an appropriate name meaning simply 'steep hill'. Its rugged form dominates the skyline for travellers on the A838, giving it an importance and grandeur out of all proportion to its height. After a few yards of road walking it is time to pick up the well-defined stalkers' path that runs back west on a rising line before turning north to Loch na Seilge. Like nearly all such paths, this one is superbly contoured, to give the maximum height gain for the minimum amount of effort. Having driven here that same morning, I stopped for a snack by the loch, which, like so many in these parts, is a real gem hidden away in a fold of the landscape. Anyone seeking an ideal spot for meditation would be spoilt in this region, and Loch na Seilge is as good a spot as any.

The stalkers' path continues its solitary journey to the south-west, eventually ending at Duartmore Bridge north of Kylestrome, while the route up Ben Stack goes off in a south-easterly direction from this point. A small cairn marks the point where most people start the upward trek, but this is really unnecessary, for one of the joys of this ascent is to pick your own way through the outcrops to the summit ridge, weaving first one way and then another as fancy dictates. Similarly, it is possible to make the ascent in about an hour, but the view, particularly westwards, is so impressive that most people will want to linger a little longer and keen photographers will find their cameras much used. Ben Stack is only 2365 feet (721 m) high but what is important in the far north is the relative distance which is always more impressive. Hence, the height gain between Loch na Seilge and the summit is over 1640 feet (500 m), and during this ascent the landscape becomes spread out in a vast three-dimensional panorama. Initially, the path is quite boggy, so I found picking my own way upwards even more enjoyable and wondered if we are all too intent on following instructions these days. The early pioneers had neither accurate maps (the Ordnance Survey used their limited money to produce more reliable maps of urban areas rather than of unpopulated wildernesses) nor lavishly produced guidebooks. They had to rely on their appraisal of a mountain together with their own experience and trust their own judgement. Of course, this is not important in the case of modest Ben Stack, but I do suspect that most ascents, mine included, follow the usual lines. I sometimes wonder what we are missing by not making up our own minds and following our own inclinations. We should also perhaps remind ourselves that a guidebook is exactly that – a guide, not a gospel!

Arriving at the summit ridge I caught the full force of a harsh easterly wind that had been building up all day and left no room for any other thoughts as I was determined to keep to the top itself and not use the path a few feet below. I passed the true summit and then battled on to the triangulation pillar at the southern end, which is some six and a half feet (two m) lower. This is a beautiful top but is somewhat spoilt by what appears to be a private radio relay station, powered by solar panels on the very ridge itself. No doubt its use is necessary, but the siting is less than ideal. Ben Stack is an ideal vantage point none the less, with Arkle, Foinaven and Loch Stack dominating the view. Meallan Liath Coire Mhic Dhughaill is seen beyond Loch Stack, and the attraction of this shapely mountain is clear immediately. Most importantly, both the route already travelled and the way ahead can be seen from here, making the effort of the ascent most satisfying.

Loch Stack from the slopes of Arkle

•

Ben Stack to Foinaven

•

I made my way off the eastern side of Ben Stack down Leathad na Stioma aiming for the private road at the southern end of Loch Stack which leads to the estate house, Airdachuilinn, and beyond. The ground is uneven under foot and can be boggy but no one way seems particularly better than another and one of the joys of walking this far north is the lack of eroded paths. Heading downwards, there is a panoramic view ahead where the very few buildings in this landscape actually increase a feeling of remote isolation from a more populated world. A similar feeling comes from passing Airdachuilinn, which is idyllically situated by Loch Stack and where, during the winter, a number of deer can often be found in the garden. The track also gives a close-up view of Arkle and, later, a good backwards perspective on Ben Stack. At Lone the track splits, with one route going due east to Gobernuisgach Lodge some eight miles (thirteen km) away. While Cameron and I prefer not to give precise details of the locations of bothies, I will make an exception in the case of Lone. Some books imply that the bothy is an open one, but this is not the case. The building, which is securely locked, is maintained and used at certain times of the year by John Ridgway's Adventure School based at Ardmore which has an arrangement with the Reay Estate. It is not available for general use by hillgoers.

As I walked on the level ground beyond Lone my eye was caught by the small woodland ahead and the large split boulder at its entrance. In an almost surreal arrangement this boulder guards the entrance with the path going straight through the middle. After recent rain, it is worth making a brief detour to the right just before leaving the wood to see Eas Allt Horn (marked only on the 1:25 000 map), a short but impressive waterfall that carries a large volume of water when the stream is in spate.

I found the journey to Bealach Horn no less interesting than the high tops. The path rises approximately 1300 feet (400 m) but is well contoured and the Allt Horn itself is always changing as it contours around the flank of Arkle. Later, as Creagan Meall Horn dominates the skyline ahead, the most marvellous vista is revealed to the north-west where two upland lochs, Loch an Easain Uaine and a smaller unnamed one at grid reference 335454, are revealed gradually. Arriving at Bealach Horn there is a real feeling of emerging out of the confines of the V-shaped glen, and crossing the 1640-foot (500-m) contour at the bealach marks a new perspective on this whole area. Looking back to the south-west is the impressive Lochan na Faoileige occupying a splendid upland position, with Arkle's eastern ridge rising above it. There is so much visual information to take in, but it needs little time to realize that around here is a choice of prime camping spots that would serve as an ideal base for further exploration. I pitched my tent and did just that.

The next morning, in spite of Foinaven's long ridge pulling me ever onwards, I spent some time observing the rocky structure of Arkle's upper corries, which make a dramatic contrast with the rounded southern side. The route I was taking results in a long walk in to Foinaven but one that is undoubtedly worth while. Travelling through this remote area allows the mind ample opportunity to savour a constantly changing landscape and to become one with it. From Bealach Horn I went almost due north to An t-Sail Mhor. The 1:50 000 map does not show the area of peat bog that lies ahead. At first I was worried the bog might signal a rough passage and much wasted energy, but it turned out to be easier than I had feared. I kept just under the ridge on my left, making quick progress, but I was distracted by getting the first views to the east. Ben Hope (3041 feet/927 m), the most northerly Munro, is an obvious landmark about 15 miles (24 km) away. It rises in lofty isolation above the surrounding landscape, making its appearance correspondingly more impressive. Its Viking name, meaning 'hill of the bay', is especially appropriate as it towers above the slender finger of its namesake loch.

As I arrived at the ample shelter on An t-Sail Mhor my attention now turned elsewhere. To the north-east is an aerial view of Loch Eriboll around whose deeply indented shore I had driven many times. I will never forget my first visit: I approached from the east, not having properly looked at the map, and belatedly realized that a distance of under three miles (five km) separated one shore from the other yet necessitated a diversion almost ten times that distance!

Now I wandered over to get a closer view of my chief objective – Foinaven itself. The name is usually translated as 'white hill', which accords with the whitish appearance given by its quartzite rock, and its colour may well be enhanced by the contrast it makes with the browns and greens of the surrounding land. However, Peter Drummond, in his ever-enlightening *Scottish Hill and Mountain Names*, tells, if I have understood him correctly, a different story. Many writers had assumed that the name was a corruption of the Gaelic *fionn bheinn*, but local pronunciation, usually the best source of information, gives *foinne-bheinn*, which translates as 'wart mountain' – far less flattering! Certainly it is a sprawling mass of a mountain but none the worse for that. Walking west to point 808 it is not possible to see every foot of the ridge but there is no doubting its length. Running for over three miles (five km), its well-defined form maintains a course northwards while the eastern side, normally hidden from view, has three great corries scarred into it together with the unmistakable sharp A' Ch'eir Ghorm ridge. This ridge, which can be used as a bold line of ascent, is itself more than a mile long, which gives this enormous hill a true sense of scale: even the 1:25 000 OS map fails to mark all its features. Ahead of me, making their way to point 869, where A' Ch'eir Ghorm joins the main spine of the mountain, I saw two other walkers. They were the first people I had seen in two days and appeared to have come up the western slopes. Of course, it might have been a very different story if the re-survey of Foinaven

Western seas and storm clouds from the high tops of Sutherland

a few years ago had raised it to Munro status. As it is the main summit, Ganu Mór, was 'elevated' from 908 m (2979 feet) to the current 914 m. That equates to 2999 feet – almost 3000 but not quite! The missing inches are vital, yet I for one am pleased that it is not an inch higher, preferring the current peace and quiet to the inevitable consequences of being named a Munro.

Foinaven to Rhiconich

•

Sometimes I think writers like Cameron and myself are in danger of describing some features in too much detail and, in doing so, of taking away some of the mystery of our high places. In my view Foinaven's summit ridge is a place everyone should have a chance to explore for themselves, uncluttered with too much advance description and without every feature described in minute detail. Suffice to say that this particular day I had the pleasure of taking the ridge at my own pace, heading steeply down at first before crossing Cadha na Beucaich and upwards to point 869 as the mist began to wreathe around the shattered crags and highest tops. Then I continued to the true summit savouring the eagle's-eye view down to Choire Leacaich and Srath Dionard beyond, with its prominent track leading to Loch Dionard. By this time I was feeling more than a tinge of regret, for this was a trip I wanted to prolong and yet I knew that each step brought me nearer home. Sometimes it is a relief to know the end is in sight, but today I felt exactly the opposite. The final summit, Ceann Garbh, is over 2950 feet (900 m) and provides a last opportunity to look out as master of Sutherland. Glas Choir Granda, with its tiny lochan, formed the foreground beneath my feet; in the middle distance was a whole watery mass covering every point of the compass, while on a clear day the Outer Isles are clearly silhouetted on the horizon. I defy anyone not to be impressed by this scene or to be unmoved as he or she tramps from one end of the ridge to the other. Even when the views are far from perfect, this is a summit ridge full of atmosphere and grandeur.

However long I lingered at the far end, the result was inevitable and after one final look around I descended north-westwards down past Creag na Claise Càrnaich with my sights firmly set on Rhiconich. On the restricted scale of the 1:50 000 map it looks as if Loch na Claise Càrnaich and Lochan Cùl na Creige might be one continuous sheet of water. In fact they are separated by a small patch of land, and passing between them I finally joined the A838 at the bridge just north of the village. Now my thoughts were on a bed at Rhiconich's hospitable hotel, a pint or two of real ale, a good meal and a bath. Sutherland had, once again, woven a special magic and provided another fine set of memories.

CHAPTER TWELVE

CAPE WRATH

AN UNFORGETTABLE EXPERIENCE IN THE FAR, FAR NORTH
•
Richard Else

An ideal complement to the preceding walk combining a classic coastal trek to Cape Wrath with an exploration of the interior of this little-visited area

---

Map: *OS 1:50 000 Sheet 9*
Start: *Either Kinlochbervie (Grid Ref: 222564) or Blairmore (Grid Ref: 195601)*
Finish: *Just north of Gualin House on the A838 Laxford Bridge to Durness road. Grid Ref: 308568*
Length: *Approximately 25 miles (40 km), starting from Blairmore*
Approximate time: *3 days*
Terrain: *Rough walking, especially inland, but with no real difficulties, although stamina and determination may be required if the ground is wet!*
Accommodation: *Limited choice (especially so outside the short tourist season), but good hotels at Kinlochbervie, Inshegra, Rhiconich and Durness, together with b&bs and guest-houses*

Almost everyone is faced with a long journey when travelling to the far north of Scotland and, on that basis alone, it might seem sensible to include in this book a second walk in that area. So while no excuse is needed for this additional route in Sutherland, the walk is, in fact, included for another reason. The journey of 15 miles (24 km) and more from Kinlochbervie north to Cape Wrath is, in my opinion, one of the finest coastal walks in Scotland; once it is combined with a journey into the rarely visited heart of this peninsula it becomes a veritable classic. The walk is also open to a number of variations: for example, walking eastwards to the Kyle of Durness and then ascending Beinn Spionnaidh and Cranstackie, which provide a fine overview of the peninsula. This multi-day jaunt is full of variety and interest and, taken together with the previous route, gives a good selection of the many attributes of this region. Other walkers are not likely to be encountered, except perhaps at Sandwood Bay, and within the space of three or four days there are the contrasting attractions of coastline, moor and mountain.

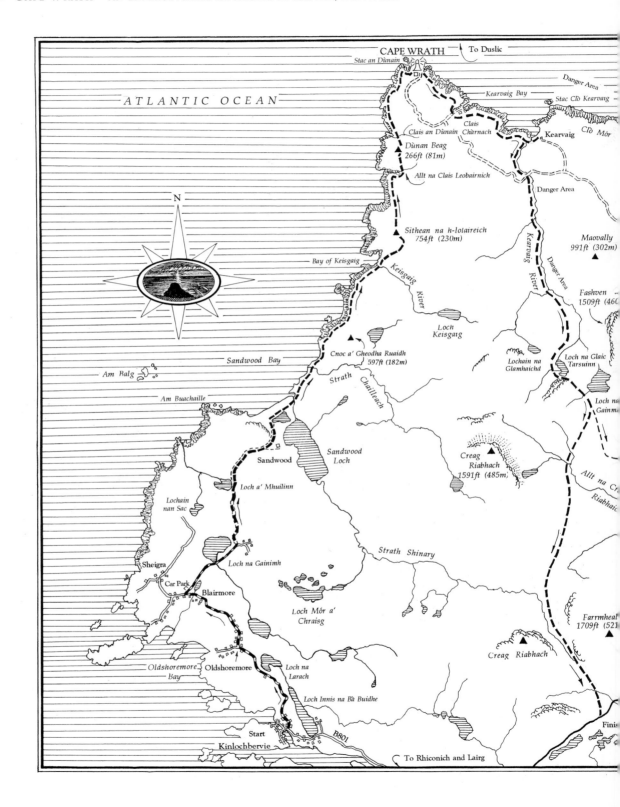

CAPE WRATH

To Duslic

Stac an Dùnain

ATLANTIC OCEAN

Danger Area

Kearvaig Bay

Stac Clò Kearvaig

Clais
Clais an Dùnain   Chàrnach

Kearvaig

Clò Mòr

Dùnan Beag
266ft (81m)

Allt na Clais Leobairnich

Danger Area

N

Maovally
991ft (302m)

Sithean na h-Iolaireich
754ft (230m)

Kearvaig River

Danger Area

Fashven
1509ft (460

Bay of Keisgaig

Keisgaig River

Loch
Keisgaig

Lochain na
Glamhaichd

Loch na Glaic
Tarsuinn

Sandwood Bay

Cnoc a' Gheodha Ruaidh
597ft (182m)

Strath Chailleach

Loch na
Gainm

Am Balg

Am Buachaille

Creag
Riabhach
1591ft (485m)

Allt na Cr
Riabhaid

Sandwood
Loch

Sandwood

Loch a' Mhuilinn

Lochain
nan Sac

Strath Shinary

Sheigra

Loch na Gainimh

Car Park
Blairmore

Loch Mór a'
Chraisg

Farrmheal
1709ft (521

Creag Riabhach

Oldshoremore
Bay   Oldshoremore

Loch na
Larach

Loch Innis na Bà Buidhe

Finis

Start
Kinlochbervie

B801

To Rhiconich and Lairg

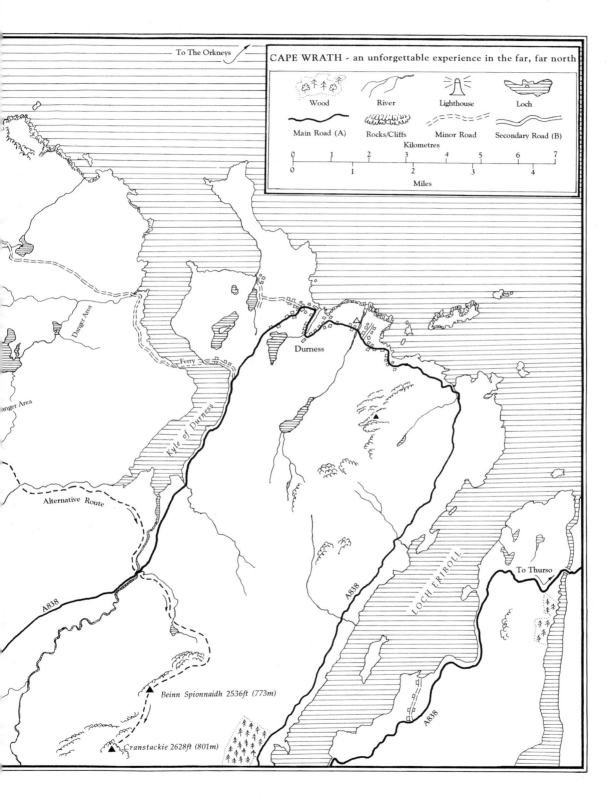

CAPE WRATH - an unforgettable experience in the far, far north

Wood River Lighthouse Loch

Main Road (A) Rocks/Cliffs Minor Road Secondary Road (B)

Kilometres

0 1 2 3 4 5 6 7

0 1 2 3 4

Miles

To The Orkneys

Danger Area

Danger Area

Ferry

Durness

Kyle of Durness

Alternative Route

A838

A838

Loch Eriboll

To Thurso

Beinn Spionnaidh 2536ft (773m)

Cranstackie 2628ft (801m)

A838

Although other writers have praised the Kinlochbervie–Cape Wrath walk, I think relatively few walkers actually undertake it. I was puzzling about this on my own journey north and thinking that the perceived difficulty of arranging transport at the finishing point (whether north or south), together with the obvious attractions of the higher mountains, might be partially responsible for this neglect. I also wondered if the red MoD Danger Area signs that cover part of this area were also a deterrent. My understanding is that the Danger Area marked on the OS maps represents an 'overshoot' zone, with the MoD using an offshore island for target practice with live ammunition. Whatever the reason, the omens were good as I made my way to Kinlochbervie. As I drove north-west from Lairg my attention was drawn to a number of birds, including a great northern diver and a buzzard, which began a train of thought that continued for the next few days. For this is a landscape that is inhabited as much by birds and animals as by humans, and although I had always been fascinated by birds and their behaviour I could never make any claims to be an ornithologist. A number of my friends were twitchers (although in the minutiae that surrounds any hobby, I understand that a twitcher is entirely different from an ornithologist), and in pondering the attraction of this I guessed that what fascinated me about bird behaviour is that it also told me something about human activity and how, for example, even subtle changes in agricultural practice can have wide implications for the bird population. I therefore looked forward to a few days where the influence of fellow human beings would be far less intrusive than in almost any other part of Britain.

Unless you're travelling by public transport (which in this part of the world means the leisurely companionship of the post-bus that runs from Lairg to Kinlochbervie) the walk really begins at Blairmore, where there is a large car park. Whatever route is taken to get here, the wide, sandy expanse of Oldshoremore Bay is worth exploring. Late evening or early morning see few witnesses to the continual smashing of the rolling breakers on its beach – in all but the calmest weather an impressive and mesmerizing sight. I also like walking through these crofting and fishing communities, where small cottages of all shapes and sizes cling precariously to the underlying bedrock. The journey north from Inverness is one of decreasing scale, so by the time Rhiconich is reached the mind has already adjusted to seeing fewer cars, a smaller number of habitations and fewer people. Sutherland may be the 'south land' of the Viking invaders, but there is no doubt that it is our own north land!

Blairmore to Sandwood Bay

I had been debating as to how much I should stick rigidly to the coastline itself on my journey to Cape Wrath and decided that this walk should not be bound by any notions of purism. Instead, I would go where I wished, making the most of the scenery ahead and exploring an area that contrasted with the high ground of Ben Stack, Arkle and Foinaven. In any case the first few miles of my walk were clearly mapped out as I followed the track from Blairmore to Sandwood Bay. Some years ago it was possible to drive part of the way and one of the most beautiful parts of this region was in danger of becoming spoilt by an ever-increasing number of tourists. In fact, this land and a number of surrounding communities, including Sheigra and Oldshoremore, form part of the 11 365-acre (4600-hectare) Sandwood Estate. Unlike some other notable estates in the far north which are privately owned and run with little, if any, concern for the wider community, the Sandwood Estate was purchased in 1993 by the John Muir Trust. I have written in the first edition of *Wilderness Walks* about the sensitive work of the trust on the Strathaird Estate in Skye and am delighted that its work here is no less exemplary. The trust takes its name from the great Scottish-born conservationist John Muir and exists for the conservation of wild places, balancing the pleasure they bring to people like myself with the needs of local inhabitants for whom they provide a livelihood. In my opinion, what marks out the JMT from other bodies is its sensitive approach to such issues, together with a desire to leave the land in as wild or as natural a state as possible. The trust is devoid of the intrusive interpretive centres, guided walks and gaudy signs that we see in so many other places. I walked into Sandwood joined by Will Boyd-Wallis, the JMT conservation manager and a fund of knowledge about the whole area. He has written a valuable leaflet about the estate (which is well worth obtaining), and he has an enthusiasm for this area which is catching. It is he who has put up the small notice at the start of the estate that says, 'Walkers Welcome', and he reminds visitors that this is a 'crofting and conservation area', demonstrating that the two roles need not be incompatible. All too often a gulf exists between visitors to an area and its inhabitants. On the one side is the argument that any precious landscape is too important to have its fate decided only by local residents, while, to put the other side of the debate, local people often take exception to outsiders interfering in what they see as their own affairs. I have spent all my adult life living in similar remote communities and have a sympathy with both viewpoints and applaud the JMT for trying to resolve these complex issues.

I am sure that all keen walkers would, if asked, say that they broadly support the concept of conservation. That, of course, is the easy bit. Far harder is to turn goodwill into positive action. In my view the challenge to organizations like the JMT is to persuade the 7000 or so people who visit Sandwood Bay each year to consider trust membership. Then some real progress might be possible.

Walking along the track that used to service the peat-cutters (of which only a very few remain), I was diverted from these thoughts by the plaintive *klee-we* call of the golden plover and the dashing flight of a merlin, with its characteristic square-cut tail. In all but the extremities of the year there always seem to be a few people making the

ABOVE: LOCH GHEODHA RUADH, NORTH
OF SANDWOOD BAY

RIGHT: THE SLIM FINGER OF AM BUACHAILLE RISING FROM
THE WATERS OF SANDWOOD BAY

four-mile (six-km) journey to Sandwood Bay and today was no exception. The walk passes a number of lochs, and immediately there is a feeling of entering a remote, unpeopled landscape, although a solitary man inhabited one of the adjacent glens until only a year or so ago.

After an hour's walking, Sandwood Loch and Bay lie ahead, with a derelict building immediately in front. This was used by shepherds until the middle of this century but recently has been the subject of some debate in the JMT. After considering a number of options the trust has decided to remove the remaining part of the roof, which is now in a dangerous state, and to stabilize the rest of the building by pointing up and capping the exposed walls with lime mortar. A relative of the last person who inhabited the building has offered a donation to complete the work. At first I was unsure about the trust's decision, wondering about the merit of spending money on simply maintaining a derelict building. But further thought, and a conversation with Will (who spoke about the dangers both of leaving the building in its current dangerous state or of restoring part of it for the trust's own use in maintaining the estate), convinced me that the trust had, in fact, made a wise and in some ways courageous decision.

Leaving the ruined building, I set out to explore the area. Although I always find something new with each visit, my eye inevitably is drawn to the magnificent slender pillar of Am Buachaille. This sandstone obelisk (whose name curiously translates as 'the herdsman') just off the coast at the western extremity of the bay stands some 195 feet (60 m) or so high, guarding the southern approach to the bay. It is separated by about 26 feet (8 m) from the coastline, and the channel between the two can be crossed in one of three ways: swimming, using a long ladder or by the first person swimming across and fixing a rope for the remaining people to use as a Tyrolean traverse. Like many other sea stacks in this part of the world, it was first climbed in the 1960s by a party that included one of the country's best climbers, Dr Tom Patey. Walking from the stack along the bay is an unforgettable experience but one that is always different, for the sand is always shifting and, in recent years, new dunes, with their distinctive marram grass, have established themselves at the northern end of the bay. A Spitfire plane, which crashed in the early years of the war, is buried on the beach, and parts of it are occasionally uncovered by the ever-moving sand. Among the waves and the salt spray it is easy to forget the other world; passing boats only emphasize this isolation. The flotsam and jetsam washed up on the beach forcibly reminded me that we are messy creatures. I would very much have liked to repatriate the toilet duck and shower gel bottles with their rightful owners!

Yet such debris cannot detract from the true spirit of place that I always find here. I am not sure how the phrase originated but to me 'spirit of place' has much in common with the philosophy of ancient peoples like the native American Indians. To me 'spirit of place' means leaving something of yourself behind in such landscapes. Watching the sinking watery sun and its steely blue reflection on the sea, or clambering among the mysterious ancient remains of dwelling-places on the northern side of the loch, gives me a true spirit of place of Sandwood Bay. No wonder so many make the pilgrimage here and often return year after year. No wonder…yet. Yet while not doubting that this is an area that will always repay exploration, I am surprised that so many visitors are drawn back to their cars at Blairmore, rather than shoulder a rucksack and head further into this remarkable wilderness.

Sandwood Bay to Kearvaig

Camping by the loch, I heard the familiar pitter-patter of rain on my tent as a shower passed over during the night. But I awoke to a superb morning, with the previous day's cold blue superseded by a warm yellow light. I said goodbye to Will in the company of redshank and oystercatchers and, leaving the Sandwood Estate, began to climb up the cliffs at the northern end of the bay. I looked back to the small rocky islands a mile or so from the coast of which the largest, Am Balg, translates as 'the belly'. From where I stood the group appears as one stubborn whaleback – a stark intrusion into an otherwise barren seascape. Now the walking was over peat and heather, with the cliffs ahead composed of Torridonian sandstone, which looks dour in gloomy weather but comes to life when it catches the sun's rays. Before long I was crossing the Strath Chailleach, watching this lovely river tumble seawards over a succession of boulders. Other writers have said that this river can be hard to cross when it's in spate and a long diversion inland may be necessary. Looking at it on this particular day I found it hard to believe and people who know this area well have confirmed that they had never found it a problem. The walking is over rough ground but is easy none the less. Here I could go as I pleased and contoured round Cnoc a' Gheodha Ruaidh on the seaward side, glancing back to watch Am Buachaille gradually receding into the distance. Once the obvious features of Sandwood Bay – its loch, the spectacular beach and its unrivalled setting – have been left behind, the landscape changes. I know some people who would describe it as featureless, and while it would be true to say that good light is needed to show off its attractions, it is never lacking in interest. I find that I must consciously ease myself into landscapes such as this and learn to appreciate both their scale and diversity. My eyes may have to work harder, but the rewards are undoubtedly there, and during the morning my attention was caught by a fox I disturbed and which vanished along the clifftops and, at the other end of the scale, by a number of newts seen among the rocks and the peat. It had been a wet spring in most of Scotland, but I was surprised by how dry the ground was underfoot. Having been prepared for a boggy walk, I was delighted to find the opposite.

CRANSTACKIE FROM FOINAVEN

•

Dropping down to cross the Keisgaig River, which runs from its namesake loch to bay, I noticed the remains of an old building (not marked on the 1:50 000 map), reminding me that this landscape has not always been so devoid of human habitation. Constructing the stone-built but roofless building obviously took some effort, but whether it served as simply a temporary shelter or something more substantial is not clear.

The river runs through a narrow gorge at this point and the crossing was easy; when conditions are slippery a short detour upstream would avoid the difficulties. The crossing made, it was followed by a long steady rise up Sithean na h-Iolaireich (whose summit is marked with a small cairn draped with lichen and which offers the first view of the coastline eastwards beyond Cape Wrath) and a height gain of about 490 feet (150 m). Dropping down gently on the northern side revealed one of the most fascinating features on this part of the walk. Nearing the depression that must be crossed before ascending to Dùnan Beag is the Allt na Clais Leobairnich (unnamed on the 1:50 000 map), which makes the last part of its seaward journey through a steep-sided gorge that resembled those found in Cornwall and the zawns in Wales. The climb in and out of the gorge is a steep one, but standing by the river and looking out to sea is an impressive sight. The vertical rock slabs that form part of the northern side are most dramatic simply because they are least expected.

The final leg of my journey northwards along this contorted, jumbled coastline led to Cape Wrath itself. I had been able the see the Cape's lighthouse at regular intervals for some time and now, as I walked towards the compound that surrounds the lighthouse, I paused to look first at the natural features of this landscape rather than the man-made ones. I was impressed by the isolated steep rocks of Stac an Dùnain which nestle up to the Cape itself and which take the full force of the restless Atlantic Ocean. Even on a calm day I have noticed a strong swell around the base of these rocks, which form a wild home to numerous sea birds including fulmars – although found in great numbers today, they were proved to breed here only at the end of the last century. A splendid arch carved out by the water can be seen from further around the headland, but for the moment my thoughts were caught up in my arrival at this most remote corner of the Scottish mainland, where the buildings associated with the lighthouse form a vivid contrast with the landscape. For the few walkers who arrive here, this peninsula signals the beginning or end of their journey, and they make use of the minibus that runs from May to early September to take them the 10 or so twisting miles (16 km) to the end of the lighthouse road on the peninsula; from here a ferry crosses the Kyle of Durness to the Cape Wrath Hotel. Anyone making the journey north must take a brief look at the lighthouse (which was designed in 1828 by Robert Stevenson, grandfather of Robert Louis Stevenson) before returning to the comforts of civilization. The lighthouse-keepers have recently left, and the programme to fully automate operations was near completion as I walked alongside the perimeter walls.

I first came to Cape Wrath more than a decade ago. Then, as now, I found it a place with a special atmosphere. Perhaps this partly arises from the name: 'Wrath' may mean simply 'turning place', but the 'Cape' part of the name is what's important. It is the only such cape in Scotland and, in my romantic mind, is associated with those other famous capes – Cape Horn and the Cape of Good Hope. Throughout the ages seafarers have rounded these capes to discover a different world, and I wondered if that was the case with the Viking raiders who must have surely passed Cape Wrath and discovered the contorted, magical coastline of western Scotland.

A cold easterly wind prevented me from indulging these thoughts any longer and, with a cursory glance to the tiny sea-drenched skerry of Duslic, I headed into the fierce wind as I started my journey along the northern coast where previous views to the Butt of Lewis were now replaced with those of the Orkneys breaking the horizon out to the north-east. The next part of my journey was new and fulfilled a long-held promise to explore this area in more detail. I had once had a close-up look from the comfort of a helicopter, and now with a real feeling of excitement I began to explore on foot. I dipped down into the deep cleft of Clais Chàrnach, where one solitary worker was busying himself at the jetty that is still used periodically to bring in fuel to power the lighthouse generators. Then it was across a succession of peat hags and stark upland lochans before my final objective for the day came in sight – the beautifully curved profile and sandy beach of Kearvaig Bay. Nestling right up to the Ministry of Defence's Danger Area, its pure turquoise sea, foaming breakers, extensive bleached sands and Stack Clò Kearvaig, with its huge chockstone perched precariously between twin spires, make this one of the little known delights of the far north. At Clò Mór, around the eastern extremity of the bay, a series of impressive sea cliffs reach a height of 918 feet (280 m), making them the highest sea cliffs on the British mainland. It was now late afternoon, so I put up my tent under a clear and open sky and welcomed the ever-rolling waves as my companions. Although it was now May, I noticed that the nearby bothy had only two entries in its visitors' book this year and felt that anyone who made the effort to walk here could hardly fail to be awed by the grandeur and majesty of the place.

Kearvaig to Gualin House

The next morning I was loath to leave but after a final walk across the bay I began tramping upstream by the Kearvaig River and started my journey into the interior. The river forms the western boundary of the Danger Area (which is now shown more accurately on Ordnance Survey maps), and once I entered the V-shaped valley I thought the bay had vanished for good, only to be rewarded by a final view of it from higher up. The walking was now in complete contrast to the previous days, and I had wondered if it would prove disappointing. In fact, such fears were ill-founded, and once I had passed the garish MoD yellow and black range hut by the road bridge (the hut controls traffic flows on the road when firing is in progress) the landscape began to unfold before me in a way reminiscent of the most remote parts of the northern Pennines. Like the rolling, little-frequented hills of north-west Durham, this is a land of moor and peat bog but no less interesting for that. The Kearvaig River of brown peat runs over a bed of red sandstone, and the hills of Maovally and especially Fashven look tempting but out of bounds in the Danger Area. They would provide the kind of overview of this region that presently is offered only by hills like Beinn Spionnaidh and Cranstackie to the east of the A838 Durness road. Today, the MoD warning signs are faded and there is a temptation to ignore them, but this area is still in periodic use by the military and the rules about such trespass are unambivalent. In any event a walker who suffers a mishap is unlikely ever to be found in this wild landscape.

Making my way alongside the river and later walking south-west to the remote Lochan na Glamhaichd and Loch na Glaic Tarsuinn it was obvious that virtually no walkers ever pass this way. I wondered if, without the Danger Area and its forbidding signs, this peninsula would be more popular with walkers but doubted that this would ever be true. I know of some hardy walkers who find being on anything but the high hills a mental torture and who have a positive allergy to even the mention of moor-land and peat hags! I think it is a pity that such people have not explored this region, which has its own distinctive character. Here, the small brown trout are undisturbed in the becks, there is a virtually unparalleled feeling of space and the silence is immense. With the sun highlighting the yellow grasses that are so typical of Sutherland in early spring and a blue sky with pure white clouds overhead, this is a place that takes some beating. Around the inland lochs centred on Loch na Glaic Tarsuinn are superb places for wild camping. Here I watched a stunning broken grey-blue sky with drifting clouds and a shower of rain make way for the sun streaming in over the hills and setting the loch ablaze with endless patches of reflected light.

From here a number of options are possible, including an ascent of Creag Riabhach which, at 1591 feet (485 m), is the highest peak in the area. For example, if a car has been left at Blairmore, it is possible to return by climbing Creag Riabhach before walk-ing westwards to Sandwood Bay and out along the track. Whichever route is chosen it will involve, in all but the driest conditions, some wading through peat bogs, although careful planning will avoid the worst excesses! My particular route was not the most direct but had other merits. I passed to the east of Loch na Gainmhich and, heading south, found the walking rough with the possibility of sinking into the bog – often without any warning! Looking across to the imposing cliffs on the north-east of Creag Riabhach was a real surprise: they are around 656 feet (200 m) high, approximately a mile (one and a half km) long and the three rock-climbing routes that were put up here in the 1970s may still be waiting for a second ascent! By now I was heading due south into the base of the glen and crossed over the Allt na Creige Riabhaich, which is just wide enough to be difficult after heavy rain. I was walking in the middle of a vast amphitheatre, and now the going was hard under foot. Yet I found the landscape and a translucent quality of light more than made up for the effort expended. Crossing the watershed, I passed between Creag Riabhach on my right and Farrmheall on my left and then, suddenly, the walk was almost over. Two prominent radio masts reminded me of the everyday world as I came over the bealach and, a short time later, started to drop down to the main road. This is a part of Scotland where often only one vehicle will pass every five or ten minutes but where, in consequence, hitching a lift is incredibly easy. With the sort of culture shock that is sometimes experienced when visiting foreign countries, I was back in my hotel and having a shower less than an hour later and, shortly afterwards, enjoying a beer.

In trying to sum up my thoughts on this wild landscape I climbed to the top of Cranstackie a couple of days later and had a panoramic view over this landscape of rock and water framed by two concentric rainbows. Tomorrow I would be heading back home to Inverness-shire, a three-hour journey south to the heart of the Highlands and to an entirely different world. On previous visits I had always made a promise to return to this part of Sutherland sooner rather than later and today was no exception. For in the whole of Scotland, with its tremendous variety of mountain scenery, there is nothing remotely like the land now laid out beneath me. Judged by any standards it is unique, somewhere in which to devise your own itineraries and to explore patiently and at length. An ideal setting, in fact, for a real wilderness walk.

SUMMER RAINBOWS NEAR THE SUMMIT OF CRANSTACKIE

•

POSTSCRIPT

IN THE HILLS AGAIN

•

Richard Else

While describing the routes in this book I have, once again, inevitably been thinking about the walking 'bug'. I have been pondering about why long wilderness walks have become such an important part of both my own and Cameron's life. We have both been walking for so long that sometimes it is hard to actually recall the many individual processes that have led to what motivates us today.

Recently we both had the pleasure of Hamish Brown's company when we filmed with him in Morocco's High Atlas Mountains. I have long admired Hamish and was enthusiastic about being shown these unfrequented mountains. Gradually, we made our way up from the bustle of Marrakesh to the quieter country town of Taroudant. Then the journey began in earnest as we travelled in two Land Rovers up the rich Medlawa Valley to where the road ended at Tagmout. Finally, we started a walk that took us progressively higher, passing through a number of small communities where foreign visitors are almost never seen, until we completed the dozens of zigzags that make up the Tizi n' Targa. This high mountain pass leads to the Ticka Plateau, which is feared by local people who regard the mountains as a dangerous place. In such country the overwhelming feeling, apart from the genuine friendliness of the local inhabitants, is of exploration. Once the plateau is reached, an enormous vista opens out which reveals mountain after mountain, peak after peak. Within this one region months could be spent climbing hills that have had only a few, if any, ascents. Alternatively, it would be inspiring to link them together and form an imaginative and demanding traverse. Our particular objective was a fine, shapely mountain called Imaradene. Standing on its summit I found difficulty in believing that it had probably had fewer than 50 ascents. Real exploration! At 10 998 feet (3352 m) it is within the grasp of almost any competent and reasonably fit hill-walker.

For someone like Hamish Brown, a love of wild places, and writing about them, has been the dominating force in his life, while the majority of hillgoers will have to juggle their visits with a variety of other demands, including the need to keep body and soul together. Cameron and I have managed, in our own complementary ways, to devise a lifestyle that allows us both to live in the places that mean so much to us and to earn a living. We often ask ourselves about our relationship with the wild places and why it continues unabated year after year. The answer to what appears quite a simple question is incredibly complex. Partly there are always new places to discover, even in a country like

Scotland. That exploration is personal and differs with each individual: however well I know a glen, or a mountain, or a summit, no matter how many times I might have trodden that way before, something will always be new – on a small scale it might be a beck that has not been appreciated fully; in a wider perspective, it might be a view that has not been comprehended in its entirety. Sometimes, of course, there is the great good fortune of being in just the right place at the right time when a chance combination of weather, light and visibility offers a rare glimpse of astonishing beauty that may never be seen again and which more than compensates for days spent trudging through heavy rain.

Yet we do not go to the hills just for perfect weather, and I know that Cameron and I have never returned from a trip – whatever the conditions – without having gained some insight from it. I speak for both of us in saying that I hope this book will inspire and encourage but not confine. Levels of fitness, age or perceived ability do not matter. What matters is that just outside (literally outside my own door!) is a landscape that has the power to refresh and inspire us. It is one that, in an increasingly pressurized and arguably more sophisticated world, can reward us with true pleasure. There is nothing better after a long trip than experiencing an aching body but a rejuvenated mind. In concluding this second book of wilderness walks I would offer two observations about the themes that have been raised within these pages.

First, there is a commitment in undertaking a multi-day trip that is lacking in just a quick dash of a few hours into the wild places. Only the other evening I met two Americans who were taking part in the TGO magazine's annual Challenge (a long-distance walk across Scotland from west to east). This couple were in their mid-70s and after a long day were exhausted and slowly making their way down our glen to an overnight stop. Although tired and weary, their happiness and achievement were self-evident. Each year they maintain their trip will be the last, adding the observation: 'Your mountains are so hard.' But they keep returning year after year, and that enthusiasm should serve as an inspiration to everyone.

Secondly, I have come to the view that I personally now have to make a more positive effort to care for the landscape that has defined my life and, I hope, that of my children. In other words, we all need to make a real contribution to its preservation. In my opinion such a viewpoint is not incompatible with the needs of industry and the indigenous population, but we must all do whatever we can – no matter how little that might appear to be. In my case this includes supporting wholeheartedly the work being undertaken by the John Muir Trust and I hope others might be similarly inclined. A simple truth is now clearly evident: we can no longer take our own pleasure from the landscape and offer nothing in return. By supporting an organization like the John Muir Trust we have an opportunity to assist in the sustainable future of a landscape that is, quite literally, irreplaceable. As Muir himself wrote: 'Do something for wildness and make the mountains glad.'

Happy walking!

Further Reading

Scottish Mountaineering Club and Scottish Mountaineering Trust publications

Derek A. Bearhop, *Munro's Tables*, new edition 1997

Donald Bennet, *The Munros*, 1985

Donald Bennet, *The Western Highlands*, 1983

D.J. Bennet and T. Strang, *The Northwest Highlands*, 1990

Peter Drummond, *Scottish Hill and Mountain Names*, 1991

D.J. Fabian, G.E. Little and D.N. Williams, *The Islands of Scotland including Skye*, 1989

Peter Hodgkiss, *The Central Highlands*, 1984

Scott Johnstone, Hamish Brown and Donald Bennet, *The Corbetts and Other Scottish Hills*, 1993

Tom Strang, *The Northern Highlands*, 1982

Adam Watson, *The Cairngorms*, 1982

Other Publications

Edward Abbey, *Desert Solitaire*, McGraw-Hill 1968

Hamish Brown, *The Last Hundred*, Mainstream 1994

Hamish Brown, *Climbing the Corbetts*, Gollancz 1988

Hamish Brown, *Hamish's Mountain Walk*, Gollancz 1977

Bruce Chatwin, *The Songlines*, Picador 1987

E. Chatsworth and R. Nathan, *Stress Management*, Souvenir Press 1982

Andrew Dempster, *The Grahams*, Mainstream 1997

Ralph Waldo Emerson, *Nature*, Beacon Press, first published 1836

Richard Gilbert, *Exploring the Far North-West of Scotland*, Cordee 1994

Seton Gordon, *Highways and Byways in the West Highlands*, 1995 reprint by Birlinn of the original 1935 edition of this classic work

Hamish Haswell-Smith, *The Scottish Islands*, Canongate, updated edition 1997

Heading for the Scottish Hills, compiled by the Mountaineering Council of Scotland and the Scottish Landowners' Federation, 1988

Ray Jardine, *PCT Hiker's Handbook*, Adventure Lore Press 1996

Michael Mayne, *This Sunrise of Wonder*, HarperCollins 1995

Cameron McNeish, *The Munros: Scotland's Highest Mountains*, Lomond Books 1996

Cameron McNeish, *The Munro Almanac*, NWP 1991

Cameron McNeish, *25 Walks in the Trossachs*, HMSO 1994

Cameron McNeish and Richard Else, *Wilderness Walks*, BBC Worldwide Ltd, 1997

Roderick Nash, *Wilderness and the American Mind*, Yale University Press 1967

Jim Perrin, *Spirit of Place*, Gomer 1997

Robert Leonard Reid, *The Great Blue Dream*, Hutchinson 1992

Dr Hans Selye, *Stress Without Distress*, Hodder & Stoughton 1974

Sir Walter Scott, *Rob Roy/The Lady of the Lake*

John Thomas, *The Skye Railway*, David St John Thomas, revised edition by John Farrington 1991

Henry David Thoreau, *Walking*, Beacon Press, first published 1862

Alan Vittery, *The Birds of Sutherland*, Colin Baxter 1997

Tom Weir, *The Scottish Lochs*, Constable 1970

Andy Wightman, *Who Owns Scotland*, Canongate 1996

E.O. Wilson, *Biophilia*, Harvard University Press 1984

Paul and Grace Yoxon, *The Geology of Skye*, Skye Environmental Centre 1987

Paul and Grace Yoxon, *Prehistoric Skye*, Skye Environmental Centre 1987

Index